Worship and Spirituality

Worship and Spirituality

(Second Edition)

Don E. Saliers

OSL PUBLICATIONS
Maryville Tennessee

Worship and Spirituality
(Second Edition)

First Printing — July 1996
SecondPrinting — August 1997
Third Printing — November 1999
Fourth Printing — January 2002
Fifth Printing — February 2003
Sixth Printing — December 2003
Seventh Printing — December 2005
Eighth Printing - July 2008

ISBN 978-1-878009-27-2

This book is printed on acid-free paper that meets the
American National Standards Institute Z39.48 Standard

Produced and manufactured in the United States of America by
OSL Publications
P. O. Box 5506
Maryville, Tennessee 37802
http://www.Saint-Luke.org

The Order of Saint Luke is a religious order dedicated to sacramental and liturgical scholarship, education and practice. The purpose of the publishing ministry is to put into the hands of students and practicioners resources which have theological, historical, ecumenical and practical integrity.

Contents

To Emilie and Harold,
my mother and father,
of blessed memory

About the Cover

The cover art and lettering was inspired by the Morgan Beatus, a mid-tenth century manuscript. A "Beatus" is the name given the *Commentary on the Apocalypse* by Beatus of Liebana, an eighth-century monk who collected and edited a collage of exegetical passages from early Christian writers, especially Tyconius, an African biblical scholar. Beatus' commentary became very popular in Spain, especially when illustrated. In AD 940, a Spanish monk named Maius wrote out and illustrated the *Commentary* for his abbot.

Maius used rather bright colors and geometric, almost abstract figures to illustrate each passage from the Apocalypse upon which Beatus commented. The illustration that inspired this cover is the "Adorationof the Lamb" from Revelation 4:6-5:8.

At the center is the Lamb of God carrying the cross-staff. Around him are the Four Living Creatures, the elders and angels.

The Four Living Creatures are portrayed as beast-headed people, each holding a Gospelbook. According to thetradition, each of the four represent a Gospel. The eagle stands for John, the Ox for Luke, the Lion for Mark and the Human for Matthew. The circles beneath each creature are wheels, which are mentioned in Ezekiel's description of the four (Ez. 1:15-21).

Eight elders with musical instruments represent the 24 mentioned in Revelation 4:10. The instruments are the cithara, similar to a lute, and a timbrel-like instrument with rows of small bells. The four angels are described in the manuscript as cherubim and seraphiom and seem to hold up the whole scene.

The artist and calligrapher is Chris Visminas, Episcopal priest and an owner of C. E. Visminas Co., Ltd. who specializes in reinterpreting the wealth of Christian tradition for modern believers.

For a catalog of bulletin covers, education materials and stationery, please call 1-800-752-1429. C.E. Visminas Co., Ltd. is located at 812 Ivy Street, P.O. Box 10189, Pittsburgh, PA 15217

Acknowledgements

This book was first published as part of a series, *Spirituality and the Christian Life,* by The Westminster Press, edited by Richard H. Bell. Having been out of print for some time, a second edition was encouraged by many requests and especially by the Rev'd Timothy Crouch of the Order of St. Luke. My thanks to him and to Barbara Thompson who ably assisted me with the preparation of this edition.

Chapter Three appeared originally in a slightly different version in *Worship,* Vol. 58, No. 1 (January 1984). I wish to thank the Order of Saint Benedict, St. John's Abbey, Collegeville, Minnesota, for permission to use the material here.

Brief portions of Chapters Two and Six are adapted from my book *The Soul in Paraphrase: Prayer and the Religious Affections,* copyright 1980, 1991 Don E. Saliers. Published by OSL Publications. All rights reserved. Used with permission.

I wish to thank Charles G. Bell for permission to quote lines from his poem "Baptism."

Lines from "Choruses from 'The Rock'" are from *Collected Poems 1909-1962* by T. S. Eliot, copyright 1936 by Harcourt Brace Jovanovich, Inc.; copyright 1963, 1964 by T. S. Eliot. Reprinted by permission of the publisher.

Special thanks are due to Richard Bell, whose careful reading of the manuscript led to helpful revisions in its first edition. To several of my colleagues at Emory I am grateful for lively dialogue and thoughtful responses to the text at a critical stage in its development, especially Hendrikus Boers and Fred Craddock.

Janet Gary typed various draft manuscripts of the original book with unfailing good cheer and assisted in preparing final copy. To her and to my wife, Jane, who proofread in the midst of her own professional demands, my heartfelt thanks.

Preface To The Second Edition

In the dozen years since writing these pages, I have worshiped in many diverse local churches and led retreats and conferences in various denominations and ecumenical gatherings. There is a restlessness with conventional Christianity among those with whom I have shared such occasions. There is a hunger for something beyond "we attend church and try to lead a good life." Conversations with laity and clergy alike have convinced me that there is much to explore and to discover about relating public worship to the living out of faith in all times and places.

The word "spirituality" is frequently used to try to get at what we mean by a living faith in daily life. But the word also is confusing and vague to many, since it is used to refer to anything and everything from New Age consciousness, to insights from twelve-step programs, to psychological help with one's lifestyle — whatever that may be. Books such as Donald Evans' *Spirituality and Human Nature* open the larger relationships between spirituality and depth psychology as well as ethics. One of the aims of this book is to reconnect the word with the patterns and practices of Christian worship. In particular I wish to reclaim the necessary connection between authentic Christian worship — whether liturgically "high" or "low" — and the distinctive shape of the Christian life.

Whatever else can be said about the many "types" of spirituality in general, these pages focus on essential features of the gathered community in Word and sacrament. What about worship enables us to live our lives "in Spirit and in truth"? The "spirit" in spirituality implies life — a coming alive to the heights and depths as well as the ordinariness of being human before God. Hence, I define spirituality as humanity at full stretch before God in relation to world and to neighbor. Christian spirituality is thus our humanity at full stretch as animated by the Holy Spirit of God — coming alive to the depths and

1

heights and the ordinariness of being human in the image of God shown in Jesus the Christ.

This book unfolds the idea that worship both forms and expresses the faith-experience of the community. Worshipping God involves telling stories, singing praise and trust and hope, sorrow and joy, delight and wonder. It trains us in lamenting, confessing, adoring, and lifting our cries for the whole world. At its best, Christian worship presents a vision of life created, sustained, redeemed and held in the mystery of grace. What we do together in acknowledging God "schools" us in ways of seeing the world and of being in it. To praise and to thank God is to learn a fundamental gratitude for the gift of life. To sing heartbreak and joy is to learn truthfulness, or at least to be given the possibility of living something other than in illusion and self-deception.

Anyone struggling with the reform and renewal of worship in our contemporary situation realizes that we must confront a series of tensions. There is always a gap between what we claim authentic and faithful worship ought to do and what actually occurs in a specific community. This is related to the social and cultural ethos of where and how the worshippers live. Differences in social, ethnic, gender, and economic background always play a role in how people participate in worship. Moreover, despite the "ideal" that is presented, what is perceived is always received through the cultural modes of communication in that particular church. This means that we cannot make one specific style or tradition the norm to judge all others.

But there is also a tension between forming Christian identity and character in and through worship and the "relevance" of worship to seekers and outsiders. This is especially true of the past few years' debates between "traditional" and "contemporary" worship; but often this tension is portrayed as a dichotomy. If this book has anything to offer to this debate, it is that what is "contemporary" may not always meet the deeper needs for identity and tradition. Likewise, what is "traditional" may be itself superficial or simply done out of habit. Thus it may well be that "traditional" services of worship are not spiritually available because they lack the deeper well-springs of the larger and broader ecumenical tradition.

Every age has always had its own specific "contemporary" awareness. What people find immediately accessible or relevant may simply be passing fads, leaving another generation spiritually empty. A deepened spirituality will require a creative use of deep tradition and a sense of connection with real life. Without an ever-refreshing sense of biblical memory, we will find both worship and our everyday struggle to live faithfully diminished.

In attending to the renewal of worship we note a final tension. On the one side there is the matter of the quality and theological adequacy of the texts, the music, the ritual actions, and the depth of the memory of God available. One the other, there is always the question of the quality of our preparation and participation in the celebration of Word and sacrament. Only when the two are formed and woven together in particular communities of worship and ministry is genuine renewal possible. This, I contend, brings with it a refreshed spirituality. Only when the life of the human spirit is grounded in both the contemplation of the mystery of God and the activity of serving the neighbor and caring for the world does it truly flourish. If the Spirit helps us in our weakness — "for we do not know how to pray as we ought" — but intercedes for us with sighs too deep for words (Romans 8:26), then we can also be bold to pray and to live the refrain: "Lord send forth your Spirit, and renew the face of the earth." (Psalm 104) Let these be our guides in the pages that follow.

One

Call to Remembrance

To remember is the beginning of redemption.

HOLOCAUST MEMORIAL

Anyone who has stood in silence before the Holocaust Memorial in Jerusalem knows something of the power of memory. Those who whisper "Mother" or "Father" or a first name at that place experience the memory in a manner unknown to those whose kin were not consumed in these events, now past fifty years removed. Those whose memories are seared by the sight and smell of smoke bear the burden of remembering with their physical senses. Yet even those of us who only know by description — from someone else's stories — know the unspeakability of what the memorial evokes. But more, all who remember with tears in future times will themselves come to understand what the inscription calls forth. The horror and the hope are made present to those with vulnerability and the courage to remember.

We live in a world that makes this particular form of remembering necessary. The long list of names Americans pass by on that mirror-like black wall in Washington is an other example. There too, in its own particularity, the wall and the words evoke in collective and individual memory the jungle war in Vietnam: bravery, suffering, death, obscure defeat, and a contemplation of the human prospect. We gaze at the wall and see our own image. Without such places and such occasions of memorial we lose something essential to our humanity — truthful recollection and sharpened hope. In such times and places of awareness and recognition, a human future becomes possible.

Not all such remembrance of pain and suffering leads to worship and the spiritual life. Indeed, many have argued that such considerations lead to the end of worship, that the enormous suffering and indignity of certain recalled events questions the very idea of God and threatens to subvert religious belief and life itself. Still, these reflections on worship and spirituality must begin precisely with the reminder that, *without* the history of suffering and death, worship of God and all religious life remain superficial. Among the necessary requisites for worship and spirituality are these: a sense of wonder and the awareness of suffering and death. These always and everywhere involve memories and take public form in common acts of commemoration. Not all worship involves remembering the experience of pain, whether of others or our own, nor can all of worship be summed up by the phrase, "sense of wonderment at the mystery of things"; but these are indispensable. No surprise that we have difficulty finding our way to authentic Christian worship and life when our lives and our culture are full of forgetting and self-preoccupation. In our best moments we know this more than we care to admit.

Communal Memory and Identity

Remembering is essential to our sense of identity. Our deepest emotions are intimately linked with how we remember and what we recall. This is why the literal loss of memory by persons in the grip of disease or struck by physical accident has such tragic dimensions. Disoriented stares from those we love, who cannot remember their own names or their relationships to persons, places, and events, are profoundly disturbing. We rightly fear the severe loss of personal memory. With such loss the world shrinks and changes. It is frightening to think of becoming a prisoner in one's own immediate experience. It is equally disturbing to think of such imprisonment without disease or accident. Books such as Christopher Lasch's *The Culture of Narcissism* give us some clues as to how this may be not only a matter of individual physiological deterioration but a social and cultural reality.

5

Without the capacity to remember, we lack a sense of narrative about our lives and our world. It is true that all human remembering in the ordinary situations of our lives involves a selecting out of the whole experienced past. What we remember may be distorted and warped by our present desires, driving passions, or compulsions. This must be admitted at the outset. The ordinary sense of "remembering the past," whether individually or collectively, is a function of our present state of mind and soul as well as a construction of the deeper aspects of our imagination. Recall your own experience: how different is your description of the details of the accident from that of the person driving the other car.

Our memories can be misleading, even deceitful at times. There are questions here quite beyond our immediate focus. Whose remembering is to be trusted, and why? Can we correct misremembering, and how? Does not all memory involve more than the simple recall of what has been personally "experienced"? For our present purposes, such questions must be kept on hold. Nevertheless, as we shall see in detail, the forms of remembering that are essential to Christian worship, prayer, and life involve precisely a critical "call to remembrance." The struggle of true with false prophecy requires facing the conflict between differing accounts of how and what is to be remembered.

Yet for all our awareness of such problems, the central issue bearing upon the relationship of Christian worship and spirituality for this book is the necessity of the communal memory of those gathered about the font, the book, and the table. Without living remembrance of the whole biblical story there would be no authentic worship, nor could there be such a thing as becoming a living reminder of Jesus Christ for others. Seeking God and embodying holiness in our whole existence depends, in great measure, on receiving and exercising the memories of the Scriptures in and through particular forms of communal traditions. Living our lives open to God requires dwelling in a common history, the narratives, the writings of the prophets, the witness of the apostles, and the extended memories of the community praying and living in accordance with them through time.

Stories of creation, covenant, and redemption, visions re-called, encounters proclaimed, prophecies uttered, God's mercies celebrated — all these are part of the corporate memories of a religious tradition. So when the child asks the ritual question at a Passover Seder, "Why is this night different from all other nights?", the answer comes in the form of a story recalling the deliverance of the children of Israel from bondage. And to the faithful it is this very night in which those gathered about the table who share the story are now delivered to freedom again. So also with the reality of Jesus' words, "Do this in remembrance of me."

For any of us who seek God in worship, the interior of our own lives must be open to such remembrance. Augustine provides a definitive starting point concerning our own individual lives before God. In the *Confessions,* Book Ten, we read, "But where in my memory do you abide, O Lord?" God dwells in the human memory — an astounding claim! There is no final definitive an-swer to Augustine's prayerful question. Yet he shows us how inward recollection moves us toward God; because we have remembered with God's word, we are drawn to seek God deep within.

To remember, in the sense of which the *Confessions* speak, is to call into active presence the totality of my life — not merely the "remembrance of things past" as reverie. All specific remem-brances, whether painful or joyous, of persons, places, and experiences are a kind of stairwell toward something never given in any single memory. We are to remember not a time but, rather, to consider the origin, the very beginning of our existence. Since living through time bears us continually away from our birth, rec-ollection of our lives is required in order to come back to where we began. But we began without awareness or recognition. To be drawn after God in such recollection of our lives allows us to visit the place of our origin and our destiny and know it for the first time. In this way Augustine not only retraces experienced events but also summons an awareness of our having received life as a gift. Such an interior awareness is part of what authentic com-munal memory prompts.

7

The mysterious connection between learning to worship with the community of biblical memory and the opening up of these interior dimensions of our lives is the subject of the remainder of this book. In this way remembering is constitutive of faith itself and not a mere elaboration of beliefs already held. In asking God to remember us and by invoking the Spirit to aid us in remembering who God is, we touch on the paradox of how the past becomes radically present. The forms of being called to remembrance of what has taken place between God and our stories in the past give us a future as well. This suggests that authentic biblical worship is a peculiar kind of "future present," but always grounded in the mystery and suffering of real human history.

Here is a decisive point in the initial stages of our reflective journey. We must speak of more than memory in the general run of human life. Our aim is to explore *redemptive memory*. What is true of our common experience as human beings — the joy and grief, the pity, despair, and hope — these deep emotions and abiding features of our common lot are to be given a new shape and a particular content. In worship, prayer, and the life of compassionate discipleship, remembering with the Scriptures over time and in all circumstances is to turn in a new direction. We live, feel, intend, and understand the world differently because a shared biblical memory forms in us an awareness and disposition oriented toward the mystery of God. Entering the patterns of redemptive memory with the people of God risks conversion.

These facts invite reflection upon how, in Christian worship and spirituality, remembering God drives us toward a radical becoming.

Some have thus spoken of the "dangerous memory" of Jesus Christ.

Biblical Remembering

In turning to the forms of remembering in the Bible, we make a startling discovery. Our modern idea of memory as recalling past events or re-examining fixed history is called into question. Biblical remembrance, while including such matters, is above all a shock of recognition. Essential to the worship in Israel, early and late, is the movement between "Israel remembers" and "God remembers." On the one hand, in the commemorative actions of keeping alive their past history with God, the people of Israel were involved in something beyond mere psychological recall or vague historical projection. "To remember Yahweh" is the central identity-giving corporate vocation of the gathered assembly. By reciting what God had done in creation, in deliverance from bondage, in covenant, Law, and prophecy, Israel's true identity and destiny were made real and revealed anew. The primary aim of worship in the cycles of festivals and seasons was to actualize the tradition.

Of course this remembering was obvious to any who had themselves, or within living memory, seen and heard the great works of Yahweh. But when exile and centuries intervened, a deeper aspect of communal remembering emerged, especially expressed in Deuteronomy. There the writer's concern is with a later generation, a people who did not go through the waters or participate in the redemptive exodus from Egypt into the promised land. Thus Deuteronomy confronts an issue fundamental to all biblical faith: How can a people still live from saving acts in the past if they are separated by many generations from these definitive events? Telling the stories? Yes, but that alone was not sufficient. Not by mere nostalgia nor by a psychological reliving of these past times could the biblical meaning of trust in God be made real to subsequent generations. Rather, there had to be a contemporary encounter, a vivid recognition on the basis of what was remembered, that God was now encountering Israel anew in the present experience — in the very exile or suffering, or in whatever time and place forced them to remember. So they, in thanksgiving and in lament, called upon God to "remember." This is the heart of biblical spirituality and worship. Singing the psalms is a part of becoming God's people anew.

"Hear, O Israel," proclaims and invites the *Shema* of Deuteronomy; "the Lord our God is one Lord, and you shall love the

Lord your God with all your heart, and with all your soul, and with all your might." When the children ask the meaning of God's commands, the historical tradition of Israel's redemption is retold, and the very present moment of worship becomes the place of encounter and dialogue with a living God. To remember what God has done — if we pray with the Bible — carries the astounding claim that what God said and did, God still says and does. The redemptive presence and power of God is intimately linked with the very acts of acknowledging, invoking, and supplicating God's mercy and memory. The very capacity to remember and retell the history is itself a sign of God's ongoing life in the community's midst.

To pray to God in any and every circumstance is thus to remember and hence to invoke God's presence now, and to seek God's mercy and loving-kindness afresh. Again and again the psalmist cries, "Remember your people, which you have redeemed.... Remember not our sins" (Psalms 25, 51, 74, 79). At the same time, Israel is commanded to obey God's precepts in order to remember that redemptive history in daily life. To remember to keep the Sabbath Day holy is thus a way of participating in the continuity of the creation and redemption which God always intends. What God was for Israel, God still will be. But that fact can only be grasped in the joyous and the painful remembering. The psalms of lament as well as the hymns of thanksgiving and praise form a continual song of remembrance of who God is and who God promises to be. Whether in blessing God or in crying out in distress or utter desolation, such remembering is an active encounter. "Bless the LORD, O my soul, and do not forget all his benefits" (Ps. 103:2); or Job's cry, "Remember that my life is a breath" (Job 7:7); or "Do not remember the former things" (Isa. 43:18) — all these are part of the whole emotional range of the vocative. The language addressing a living God in every human situation signals a deep conviction and trust that God is present even when God seems absent.

So the remembering of Israel is itself a communal act and hence is also an act in solitude, a present dialogue and encounter with the living history of God's redemptive presence. "He has remembered his servant Israel," sings Hannah, and Mary in her prophetic song as well. Psalm 105 presents another powerful example of a song that calls Israel to thankful remembrance of God's mighty acts, which are even now present to and in the midst of the faithful: "Remember the wonderful works that he has done."

The psalms, which are so central to Israel's worship and to the whole range of Christian worship, form and express us in that same emotional range of memory. Christian liturgy, from the early Church to Calvin to the *Book of Common Prayer,* is permeated by those images and living lines of prayer. Individual and communal praises, hymns, and laments are always before God who is remembered. To recall and even to express vivid alienation, exile, and rejection is *not* mere self-indulgence or pious sentiment. God is remembered and sought out. As Brevard Childs has shown so convincingly in *Memory and Tradition in Israel,* "To remember is to grasp after, to meditate upon, indeed, to pray to God" (p. 61). To remember God is to actualize the past and to gain a hope. Israel's worship and her call to remembrance in liturgy and life expressed "the process by which late Israel made relevant the great redemptive acts which she recited in her tradition" (pp. 74-75).

Part of our present diminished Christian spirituality is to be found just here: in our lack of awareness and recognition of this indelible feature of biblical faith. Not to be remembered by God is a profound threat to humanity. For the biblical writers, not to be remembered has the force of death. In Isaiah 23:16 and 65:17, for example, we note that to be remembered no more by God is to be cut off from the land of living, from identity, history, and thus from life itself.

Few of us have reflected on the depth of this insight, and our preaching and praying and singing and celebrating pass it by: Israel remembers God and God remembers Israel. Forgetting Yahweh is not mere spiritual laziness or emotional dullness, it is an act of worshiping false gods. Forgetting God's commands is a matter of breaking them by not nurturing the attitudes, emotions, and dispositions in light of God's presence: the love of God and neighbor. Forgetting the orphans and widows, for example, and any who are in need, is linked to forgetting God. To neglect justice, not to love kindness, not to walk

11

humbly with God are themselves a forgetting of God. This is part of what Jesus meant in summarizing the Law and the Prophets in the double command to love God and neighbor as God has loved us. To fail to remember "other" is the same as actively forgetting God. This point is essential to any understanding and recovery of the inner connection between worship and ethics. We will say more of this in the following chapters. For now it is sufficient to observe that spirituality can never be divorced from ethics and from the service of God and neighbor in the world of suffering and need. To separate holiness and godliness from doing the works of mercy is unfaithful to the biblical reality of remembering God in worship and in history.

The extraordinary feature of the biblical picture of God is, of course, that God will remember God's people. In Hosea we hear, "How can I give you up, O Ephraim!" God has covenanted not to forsake us, not to leave the created order to its own devices. In remembering us and all those in any adversity, God acts out of the compassion and covenant with which the whole creation was loved into being. Our lives in faith can only, in gratitude and response, seek to manifest that reality to others.

Like all generations before and after us, we need to learn the remembrance of God and to call upon God to remember us even in our seeming God-forsakenness, in the midst of our own growing kingdom of death and death-dealing. In thanksgiving we remember that God's promises are faithful; in repentance we petition that God will not remember our sins against us — will "blot out" our transgressions, as in Psalm 51.

Remembering Jesus Christ

These powerful features of biblical remembering come over into the New Testament and are given focus in the life and death of Jesus Christ. So "to remember our baptism" is to recall that we are part of a whole redemptive history. As in The Second Letter of Paul to Timothy, the Christian community is called to "remember Jesus Christ, risen from the dead, a descendant of David" (2:8). The Christian assembly and the whole liturgy of our prayer and work in daily life is to remember Jesus Christ. To be a living reminder of Jesus Christ in all that we do is the central task of Christian spirituality. For our serving others and our worship of God is to be in conformity with the image and pattern given in Christ. To remember Jesus is the same pattern that Israel's memory took in recalling the "mighty deeds" and in participating in the redemptive history itself. It is no accident, as we shall see, that the Jewish prayer forms of the *berakoth* (prayers of blessing and thanksgiving) underlie all the Christian eucharistic prayers. To worship God "in the name of Jesus Christ" is to pray to God by calling to mind and enacting in our worship *all* that has been given to us in his life and suffering and death and resurrected life. This is the heart of all Christian worship and spirituality: our participation in the mystery of his dying and rising.

Christian spirituality has lost its roots. We have forgotten that the Christian faith, grounded in Jesus, is in continuity with the people of Israel — with the whole redemptive history of God's remembering. At the same time, Christians cannot claim to have the same lived history as the Jews. We are "adopted sons and daughters." People who share a common history of suffering cannot simply be "presumptively" remembered by those who do not share that specific social identity and who may even have caused part of the suffering! Christian liturgical remembering must be humble and self-corrective.

Such practicing of liturgical memory will take us into new and difficult places. For within patterns of Christian worship we also inherit forgetfulness of women in the biblical and liturgical traditions themselves. Humility requires an honest rediscovery of women's voices **not** remembered. In our own time, the "call to remembrance" includes painful memories of women who died "surrounded by silence or contempt," but who are, in Heather Murray Elkins' words, "worthy, yes worthy!" (*Worshiping Women*, p. 20)

No authentic spiritual life can exist unless our worship and our faith and our way of life spring from the same source in God. Such worship and living is grounded in the fundamental pattern of memory and witness given in Scripture and the central Church tradition. Is it any wonder that Jesus' words and actions at the table, "Do this in remembrance of me" (I Cor. 11:24), must come to occupy more than our passing attention or momentary mental effort? The holy meal can never be fully understood or received as the mystery of God's self-giving as an individualistic act of subjective memory or feeling. The celebration of this meal requires the gathered community about the table with the bread and wine, with the recital of the whole history of God with us, and with the full, active, and faithful doing of this commemoration. This, in turn, asks of us the deepest levels of our soul and life. The Word must possess us "as though for the first time." Such a feast of God's self-communication in the human words and sign-actions requires participation in the living memory and symbols of the community.

We can never receive what Paul meant by "as often as you eat this bread and drink the cup, you proclaim the Lord's death until he comes" (I Cor. 11:26) until we enter into the mystery and the pain and the hope and joy of such living symbols and memory. How may our lives today be once again faithful to the biblical call to remembrance? Where are the sources of such recovery? Where are the communities of men and women of memory and celebration in which this becomes a way of life? I have no easy answers, but we have begun the journey, and the road beckons us on. So we turn now to worship as responding to God, and then to the "hidden languages" of symbol and sacramental participation that are waiting to touch and transform our humanity even now. But the vulnerability to God and to neighbor must dawn upon us, and the resistance to God's memory of us must be broken down.

Two

Responding to God
in Perplexing Times

What life have you if you have not life together? There is no life that is not in community, And no community not lived in praise of GOD.

> T. S. Eliot
> "Choruses from 'The Rock' "

The question "What life have you?" is an increasingly urgent one for many people whom we are called to serve. It is a question pressed upon us by the lacerations and fragmentation of contemporary life. It is a cry walling up in the hearts and lives of human beings, both inside and outside the churches. It is asked of the churches by people in the streets; but also by persons who, seated comfortably for years in the pews, are quite familiar with the language of Zion. In either case it addresses us directly: in our songs, words, actions, and gestures we have often been considerably less than a community "lived in praise of God."

In his famous book *The Shape of the Liturgy*, Dom Gregory Dix reminds us (p. 741) that "the study of liturgy is above all a study of *life*.... Christian worship has always been something done by real men and women, whose contemporary circumstances have all the time a profound effect upon the ideas and aspirations with which they come to worship." The Scriptures themselves grow out of the experience of worshiping people whose lives and songs were double testimony to life before God. In both Old and New Testament alike, the mixture of awe and human terror, of divine compassion and human hope, is sounded in the songs and worship of those called out by God. Scrip-

15

ture is a record of God's mighty acts, but it also records the ongoing life journey and experience of people called out in response. It witnesses to a God making self-revelation to a creation lovingly fashioned yet so far fallen from God's creative intent that it cries for redemption and restoration. The song of earth and the song of heaven seek each other on the lips and in the lives of real men and women from generation to generation.

The study of spirituality in the context of worship and life must always take these matters with seriousness. The divine initiative calls forth a communal response that finds its own best being in praise of its creator and redeemer. Yet the shape of that praise lives and unfolds over time. Thus, the forms, patterns, and theological content which we call "tradition" are understood and freshly received amid the ever-changing historical, cultural, and social features of existence that characterize real women and men in every generation. *Merely* to sing the songs of Zion is not enough. John Berryman's one-liner comes to mind: "We know you're there, Lord; the sweat is — we're here."

In the paragraphs that follow, I address three main points: first, the contemporary situation in which we struggle to illuminate and understand the nature of worship; second, some theological fundamentals; and, finally, some basic experiential features of worship and their implication for authentic Christian spirituality grounded in liturgical action.

The Nature of Worship in Our Contemporary Situation

There can be little doubt that we are now living through a period of great turmoil and often great confusion concerning Christian worship. Congregations have become visibly polarized or split into several grudging factions over what constitutes true worship. Many wish to do away with the old forms and language in the name of relevance and creativity; others regard any such change as tampering with "hallowed and sacred" tradition (in some cases scarcely a hundred years old). Those of us given pastoral responsibilities, both clergy and laity, often find ourselves caught in the cross fire, struggling for integrity and understanding. We live in a time of immense liturgical change, resulting from both cultural and theological pressures. Not since the Reformation and Counter-Reformation has there been so much widespread concern for the reform and renewal of inherited rites and assumed patterns, in both liturgical and free-church traditions.

Recently, I visited a local church that had undergone no less than four major changes in its style of Sunday worship within the past eight years. When a group of the lay leadership took me to dinner, they unloaded. Split by charismatics and non-charismatics, subject to the wildly differing styles of four pastors (each of whom stayed for less than three years), torn by wrangling between the choir, the organist, and the choir director, and unable to agree over whether they were an "evangelical church" or a "liturgical church," these folks were exhausted. The matter of *how* they were to worship and *who* they were when they worshiped and *what* the connection between their worship and their ordinary lives was supposed to be — all these were matters of personal anguish for men and women who cared deeply for their church and for the integrity of their faith. Whatever else was going on among them, I sensed a crisis of faith and spiritual life tied directly to these various tensions and disputes about common worship. They simply wanted to be nourished and opened up to the deeper stream of Christian worship and spirituality.

When we in churches in the United States attempt to think about the meaning and point of worship in our context today, our primary instinct is to speak of the problems of cultural pluralism and relevancy. Of course, we tend to make an industry out of the problems as well. We shop around for the church and the style of worship and life that fit our needs. These are very American things to do. Nevertheless, the shocks of cultural change do impinge directly upon the worshiping life of Christians, because the activity of worship is an inescapably human and cultural activity, whatever claims we wish to make about the activity of God in Word and Sacrament. Then, too, the last ten to fifteen years have been unprecedented ecumenically. Every major denomination has undertaken the task of reforming its rites in light of an ecumenically shared knowledge of the history of worship. No one could have anticipated the remarkable convergence in both theology and structural shape of the eucharistic liturgy or Holy Communion. This period of turmoil is not generated solely by the onslaughts of secular culture against the holy peace and order of the churches. Cultural pluralism also generates ecclesial sharing.

As will become clear, I regard this time of uncertainty and mutual exploration as part of a significant struggle for clarity and understanding with respect to the nature of faith and religious life in our age. Thus the current confusions, problems, and cultural demands in worship are signs of a period of religious vitality and reformulation as important as the century of the Reformation seems in retrospect. In the name of renewal, some persons have spoken of the credibility problem of worship: of the way in which believers hide behind old words and customs, saying one thing but meaning something else. Others have spoken of the "noise of solemn assemblies" as part of their prophetic critique of church life. So far as these complaints are connected with the inability of people to be at home in the songs and other forms of worship, the problems we now face are simultaneously cultural and theological. The clarification of meaning and point of worship in the contemporary world is crucial to the work of Christian theology. More to the point, understanding how to live the Christian life together in a culture of forgetfulness is at stake.

All this leads to an important word of caution. The reform of liturgy may not necessarily signal a genuine renewal of worship. "Reform" and "renewal" are different, though related, matters. All of us know that we can have a beautiful text, beautiful musical settings, the most theologically well-informed prayers, and the best of liturgical furnishings and yet still not have faithful liturgy. Some new songs — whether of classical origin or Christian pop culture — still do not take us farther than the narthex or the fellowship hall. Reformed rites do not automatically transform individual and communal lives, as many have already discovered. This cautionary note is addressed to all who compose texts for prayer and praise.

At the same time, continuing to pray and sing biblically impoverished texts that may also lack aesthetic power, no matter how seriously done, cannot guarantee a deepening of spiritual growth and discernment of what it is to be the Church today. Petrification, religious self-indulgence, and sanctification are not compatible. Hence, our concern for reform must be related directly to the deeper and more difficult matter of renewing the face of worship. In faithful worship we find our lives remembered and given fundamental orientation to God and neighbor.

Nothing has symbolized more dramatically this age of liturgical reform than the Second Vatican Council. That its first item of concern was worship took many by surprise some thirty years ago. As it turns out, concern for reform of the liturgy in Roman Catholicism touched deeply on all the important theological and cultural issues confronting the church. The intent was not simply a piece meal change but an *aggiornamento* — a re-spiriting — of the whole liturgy and the worshiping life of the church. As one commentator observed, the church was in transition to a renewed common life where rites would no longer be mechanically enacted, Scripture blindly recited but not understood, and the like. Rather, the church was in transition to a liturgy of authentic acts, worshiping in spirit and in truth. Of course the history of that transition, particularly within Roman Catholicism but across the liturgical spectrum as well, has been anything but smooth and easy.

The crisis in worship, then, is part of a larger cultural crisis that has thrown Christians back upon their own roots. We have been forced to raise fundamental questions again, but now in a new ecumenical context of dialogue and hope. Raising questions about the adequacy of our patterns and forms of worship has forced us to re-examine the relationship between Church and world, between God and humankind, and between worship and spirituality. The fact that more and more of human life is established and understood without any reference to God forces the question, "Why worship?" The prophetic rejection of human religiousness in the name of the gospel forces the question from another angle. Yet all the while the "crisis of meaning" is related directly to the *absence* of living memory, story, and ritual patterns in our lives; more specifically, to the absence of belonging to a community lived in praise of God. This situation demands that we regard Christian liturgy as *both* the expression of religious needs *and* the manifestation of a transcendent mystery of God in order to face the "crisis" squarely and honestly.

It is necessary to question the nature and significance of worship when it becomes disconnected from the realities of human existence. It is also appropriate to question whether certain ritual practices are Christian liturgy at all when they seem only to celebrate and to reinforce the cultural values of the time. In either case, we encounter a failure of faithfulness to the source and summit of Christian worship. Worship is something done in the world, but it is linked to the teachings and practices of the Christian life, which are given their articulation and formative power to shape and redirect human beings in the world. The forms and the language must be faithful to the nature of God and provide fitting modes of communication for encounter and communion with the divine life. Determining the faithfulness and adequacy of Christian worship in a time of cultural shifts is not, of course, a simple matter. Learning to remember, acknowledge, praise, and petition the God of all creation in a culture of romantic self-indulgence or cynical detachment and loneliness is indeed countercultural. Worship without mystery and a sense of suffering is neither biblical nor redemptive.

One of the most hopeful signs in the contemporary discussion of the meaning and point of worship is the recovery of the roots of Christian liturgy, pointing back to the period of the early Church leaders, known as the patristic period. The early Church itself did not regard liturgy simply as an otherworldly cult. Worship was a way of realizing and participating in the Realm of God, already come and yet to be fulfilled. So the liturgy — work of the people — was already something of the Realm of God manifest in the gathered community. My point is not to appeal to the early Church's understanding of liturgy as an exhaustive norm for judging contemporary patterns and forms. Rather, my point is that Christian worship was from the beginning something done in the world and prayer was action that involved the interaction of God and humanity.

In this sense the contemporary situation makes it easier for us to focus upon the essentials, though the problems of reform and renewal are delicate and complex. Worship is something Christians do together because it is our way of remembering, enacting, and expressing our life unto God. But worship is also a characterizing activity requiring time, space, forms, and people. Worship gives persons their life and their fundamental location and orientation in the world by virtue of language and gesture addressed to God. Worship gives expression to a story about the nature and destiny of all things. The story itself teaches us to regard all creatures in the world as God's.

The present situation calls for a rediscovery of the essentials. Reflection upon the continuities and the changes in worship and their consequences is therefore something foundational rather than peripheral. In thinking about the nature of worship in light of the foregoing, then, we do not simply apply an already systematized theology; rather, we are engaged in theological inquiry of the first order. For the language about God found in our theologies will have meaning and point only if the activities in which it is used to address God have meaning and point. The texts we sing and the musical forms we employ will flourish only so far as they faithfully serve the point of the singing.

Some Theological Fundamentals

Let us turn to some theological fundamentals concerning the nature of worship. Worship is corporate dialogue and communion with God. It is a corporate enactment by word, silence, rite, and song of the community's memories of God so as to invite the presence and power of God to come to awareness. Born as response to the divine initiative, worship lifts up what is human to the transforming and sanctifying power and presence of God. It ascribes to God the honor due God's holiness and brings human life to a new intensification before God. The worthiness of the Holy One calls forth praise and confers a dignity and honor to those whom God has created. Such dependence and interrelationship are not external features of worship but are rooted and grounded in the very nature of the divine life itself. True worship acknowledges the One who creates freely, who covenants and reaches to redeem with justice and compassion all creatures in their particularity.

Worship is always twofold: it is the action of glorifying God and the sanctification of all that is human before God. Glorifying God, giving praise, is itself a way of knowing the divine life. But this is precisely how human life comes to fullest truth and realization of what its own existence is: to discover and welcome the gift of creatureliness and to sanctify time and place and every relationship. The cry of pain and the remembrance of suffering commingle with praise and are offered together.

The bewildering variety of historical types, both liturgical and free, makes it obvious that human beings worship in and through a variety of historical and cultural forms. Worship is God-centered yet thoroughly grounded in human life; it is theocentric and anthropological at the same time. Because it is directed toward God and its native idiom is the language of address, worship involves a certain shift of consciousness away from the mundane. To address our lives in wholeness to God demands a discontinuity with ordinary life as well as a continuity. This is one reason why every period of reform and renewal has stressed the need to recover in *fullness* the corporate memories of the Church. In focusing upon and re-presenting the story of who God has been and has promised to be, we encounter anew what it means to be present to God now. This is not ordinary wisdom.

In Christian worship, joyful praise and thanksgiving are part of recalling what God has done in Christ. Worship is the communal action of presenting ourselves, in union with the universal work of Christ and all the gifts God bestows upon the human family, before the face of God. The very forms we employ in our prayers and songs of thanksgiving express this theological understanding. They are patterned after the Hebrew concept of *berakah,* the act of blessing God. Life is consecrated and brought to holiness by giving thanks to God for it. This understanding is basic to our contemporary ecumenical recovery of the theological character of all prayer.

The corporate memories of the people of God are contained in the Scriptures and in the living tradition of the Church's teachings. Thus, the reading, singing, and proclamation of the Word in the midst of the gathered community are essential. Neglect of the Word in its fullness has impoverished worship, even among those traditions who claim the Bible exclusively. The crucial element in the act of remembering is the fresh reappropriation of God-with-us. The mere "remembrance of things past" is theologically inadequate. Rather, as we claimed in the first chapter, the pattern of the texts and actions are to take us into continuing and future-oriented redemptive history. In this sense, the celebration of the holy meal can never be mere remembrance but must be a foretaste of the very Realm of God which is and is yet to come. But this remembering stands also as a prophetic rebuke of our self-serving local memory and forgetfulness.

Worship is something Christians do communally in response to God. It is done not just from religious duty or obligation (though this may be the "sociological" fact) but because it is the primary mode of remembering and expressing the Christian faith and the whole story of God in human history. In the actions of re-presenting and entering into the reality proclaimed in the story of the Scriptures, worshipers articulate their fundamental relations to one another and to the world. This is, of course, an ideal view. We are all painfully aware that not everyone who comes to worship is shaped by this language and action. Not all who say the words and participate are fully formed. "Not every one who says to me, Lord, Lord, shall enter the kingdom." This will always be a tension we must face.

But to speak of God and to address God in prayer mean that we undertake a certain way of existing: we are to be disposed in light of the claims expressed in the symbols and stories of biblical faith. We shall turn to this point again in the next section.

A further word is in order about the "givenness" of certain essential elements in Christian worship. Put most simply, these givens are: the observance of time itself as a means of memory and sanctity;

the rites of initiation (baptism-confirmation-first eucharist); the eucharist, or Lord's Supper; and the divine office, or daily services of prayer. All other forms of worship are dependent upon the defining structures of worship for the mainstream of Christianity through the centuries. In every age of reform and renewal, this basic canon helps to define the essentials once again. The Church ignores their interrelation at its peril. When they are neglected or obscured in their central significance, as has occurred so frequently in the history of Christian worship, Christian theology and spirituality suffer.

Worship Forming Spirituality

We have seen, in short compass, what some of the theological foundations of Christian worship are. But there is another way of looking at worship that has been implied all along in these remarks. Let us turn to the phenomena of the human actions involved in corporate prayer to see how certain patterns of human experience are both shaped and expressed there. These modes of prayer action should also speak to some of the deepest needs in our humanity, as well as convey the very substance of faith.

Corporate worship is, first and last, praising, giving thanks, blessing God. In the eyes of the world, this activity is utterly naive. It is speaking God's name in gratitude and thankfulness for God's very being, and for the world given to humankind. If someone gives another person a totally unexpected gift — fitted well to that person's delight and life — the primordial response is an unconditioned gesture of gratitude. Unless the world has made us fear that everything has a string attached, this form of thanking is absolutely fitting to the idea of God. It is also essential to our humanity. Insofar as worship is first and last speaking God's name in thanks and praise, it speaks to a deep human need. A life devoid of gratitude becomes incapable of receiving gifts and eventually of giving gifts. Worship continually shapes us in naming God, thereby keeping an essential aspect of the concept of God in place: Source and Giver of life and world.

But, secondly, worship is also recalling and retelling. Reading, singing, and proclaiming the Word recall who God is and what our story is. Huub Oosterhuis, author of *Your Word Is Near,* has put this point well (p. 8):

> When the Bible prays, the whole of creation is listed and the whole of God's history with humanity is brought up again. When we pray, with the Bible, we appeal to creation and to the covenant. We call God to mind; we remind God who God is and what God has done. What God used to mean for people in the past includes a promise of the future, the promise that God will mean something for us as well, that God will be someone for us.

Thus, recalling and re-presenting the story of God in relation to human aspirations, hopes, and yearnings becomes the occasion for discovery of true human identity.

Thirdly, worship is the acknowledgment of who we are in the sight of God. To address God, and *mean* what we say, is to encounter the truth about ourselves not known otherwise. Praying explores and continually reveals the difference between who God is and what we are. "My thoughts are not your thoughts . . . says the LORD" (Isa. 55:8). We are to be continually formed in the language of Isaiah in the temple: "Woe is me . . . for I am a man of unclean lips" (6:5). Yet confessing and acknowledging our rebelliousness and forgetfulness before God also fits the human features of our life. Truth in the inward parts is also part of our song. This is a connection between the attributes of God's holiness and righteousness and our own status. Worship gives us time and space to discover and express who and what we are when we are in God's presence: saints and sinners, creatures of immense worth yet alienated from our source of life. If thanksgiving, gratitude, and living memory are essential to our humanity, so too is confession and truth in the inward parts.

Finally, though by no means exhaustively, corporate prayer and worship is intercession. We are to pray for the world and its suffering.

This requires looking clearly and honestly at the world as it is. In interceding for the hurt and darkness of the world, we identify with others and express solidarity with them. This aspect of communal prayer disposes us in compassion toward others. We are to hold the world in all its actuality, up to God. In this respect, worship can never be an escape into another world. Worship and ethics belong together, even though our lives characteristically tell a different story.

In these four ways, and in others not mentioned here, Christian worship gives us capacities and dispositions essential to true humanity. Glorification of God is its primary response, but in doing this faithfully, humanity is brought to truth and sanctity. Worship is the work and service of the people of God, responding in the language of praise, thanksgiving, remembrance, confession, and intercession through time. We may think of it as a kind of rule-keeping activity of the language and central symbols of the faith. In recalling who God is and who we are, we identify the world to itself as what it yet shall be under the reign of God. It is truly a song for the beloved sounded back to its Source in the life of God by creatures who have ears to hear.

Do we not long for times and places of such freedom and mutuality? Does not the world cry out for times of rejoicing and weeping, of laughter, sobriety, and hope? This is what living that is faithful to its divine and human vocation can be. It can never be reduced to what C. S. Lewis calls "detestable good fellowship," nor is it only an instrument of therapy and human enrichment. Yet surely the One we are called upon to seek and to praise desires to give such gifts to the children of earth.

Worship must so focus upon God as to shape and form persons in holiness and true humanity. Our reform and renewal of liturgies in various traditions are beginning to open this out for us. Worship that does not provide the worshipers with the language, action, and song for expressing concrete human life unto God fails to be in spirit and truth. Because this is so, an absolute *uniformity* in text and style is no longer desirable, just as it was not in the early Church. But *unity* of praise and love is our earnest hope and prayer.

This point cannot be made casually. It is not an ordinary piece of information, nor is it a clever piece of theology. It speaks a mystery hidden from the eyes of the world, even in a world come of age. It links the activity of worship with the mystery of God's hiddenness from the plain view, from the indifferent and passionless attitude toward existence. Worship is a time and space where the language about God shapes and expresses us in such a mystery. It is a way of understanding. So we turn again and again to the ideal of that community lived in praise of God.

Three

Worship, Symbol, and Non-Verbal Languages

A live religion deals
In living symbols: so they prefer the river.

CHARLES G. BELL

Picture a late Sunday afternoon in high summer somewhere in Mississippi on the banks of a tree-shaded flowing river. All in their turn-of-the-century Sunday finery — the women in long dresses with parasols, the men in shirt and tie — the whites stand next to the black folk who have gathered along the leafy bank to witness. In midstream, waist-high in the brown flowing current, the black preacher, along with the deacon and the deaconess, supports the one about to go beneath the waters.

Listen to more verse from Charles Bell's "Baptism":

> Their untamed font of darkness. I recall one evening
> When the red sun broke through colonnades of cloud,
> And the two tides met, brown and golden, of earth and
> air–
> Light, calm and pure, and that violence of water–
> How they went down in white and moaning lamentation
> To the mud-brown flood and under, they broke up singing,
> Rolled on the earth, reborn out of death and nature.
>
> Through all the aseptic channels of the modern
> This wild release is pouring....

The mind and heart go back to that earlier baptistry in Ravenna, with its golden mosaic, its splendor of light and white robes and the waters parted, and the emerging reborn now led to the embrace of a community in waiting and to the feast; back still farther to those "awe-inspiring rites of initiation" in Jerusalem, Antioch, Milan, and Asia Minor. The linkage between the full immersion of the black community's powerful witness, even in a time of minority bondage, and the early initiation rites is indelible there. Each carries the mark of the dying and rising, and of suffering and release.

The early rites of baptism, stretching from enrollment in a rigorous catechumenate, through the water bath and anointing, to the festal eucharist and the preaching and instruction after baptism — these were a symbolic passage to a whole new way of being. With conventional social relations and normal ways of viewing the world and conceiving life forever changed, these rites are not only permeated by symbols and images but are themselves the primary embodied symbol of dying and rising in Christ.

Authentic worship needs living symbols. Living symbols focus the forces of life and death and generate meanings that take time to unfold. So generation upon generation who have celebrated the word and symbolic action of a Passover Seder suddenly foregather in a hidden room where a community has come secretly under the threat of Nazi discovery. The bread broken and cup shared by peasants in some violence-torn village in Central America suddenly manifests the power of symbols to carry life. Going down to death, being reborn to life, bathed in the waters of cleansing and anointing, being illumined with that reality which "no eye has seen, nor ear heard, nor the human heart conceived" (I Cor. 2:9) — all these are signified and participated in by worshipers who know the hidden languages. Should our children ask what baptism or the Passover or the eucharist means, we should say, "All of these things, and more which still remains to be lived." If cultured inquirers in our society ask, we should say the same, even though we may not fully comprehend because of the limitations of our own privileged cultural situation. It is this way with symbols in the context of authentic ritual action. As with poetry and literature, the symbols in living liturgy mean more than they say, and they present to human beings much more than what appears. This is the nature of signs become symbols. What we can think and say about the symbols can never exhaust the meaning, particularly as these are part of the sign-actions of the gathered religious community. Indeed, as Charles Bell's verse tells, a living faith deals in living symbols. This is what concerns us now: to explore various dimensions, verbal and nonverbal, of symbol and symbolic action in the ongoing worship of God's people. Spirituality is the way we live out the realities symbolized. Thus is given to those who know the memory of suffering in their own lives a more acute possibility of finding life interpreted by the symbol of the exodus or of the cross.

It is one matter to describe and interpret the efficacy of symbol in our worship and spirituality, and quite another to participate in a community of faith enacting its relationship to God and to others. Yet, while talk about symbol can never be substituted for participation in symbolic action, we must explore the prospect and possibility of deepening the human capacities for symbol in worship and in life. For more often than not, our local churches are starving for such participation; and worse, we may not even be aware of our spiritual anorexia.

Beginning with the examples already touched upon, let us examine the nonverbal dimensions of symbol in worship in light of the essentials mentioned in Chapter Two. Then we shall turn to the main thesis of this chapter: that participation in authentic liturgy requires learning the hidden languages of worship — time, place, sound and silence, the visible, and the bodily gestures belonging to narratives of creation, redemption, and consummation. Then we may draw out implications for a deepened spirituality.

How we preach and pray and celebrate the mysteries of faith is an expression and a vulnerable exposure of what we believe about God and the world. For what are we prepared to live and die? This is precisely why conventional patterns of worship and prayer often no longer satisfy people looking for honest encounter, a more sustaining memory and hope, and integrity of emotional range concerning the Christian gospel. At the same time, our culture has, despite our technological surfaces, developed a new sense of symbol, myth, and imaginative image. This is why any Christian liturgy that is merely verbal — with only the perfunctory uses of sounds, signs, words, gestures, and space — will, in the long run, fail to satisfy the deeper hungers of response to God and encounter with truth. Such conventional worship may fail the very cultural communication forms which make faithful liturgy possible. Signs and images may remain what we have conventionally taken them to be, never to become living symbol.

Beyond Words Alone

One of the most telling insights gained in recent years is that worship is basically nonverbal. This rediscovery of the essential nonverbal or "action" character of liturgy is both theological and cultural. Its recognition by mainline white Protestants has understandably been greeted with smiles of indulgence by many black and ethnic minorities. The dialogical and nonverbal character of much of the symbolic communication in many of these traditions is finally coming to be appreciated. The formative and expressive power among black Pentecostals, for example, is not something they have to rediscover. At the same time, the language used in the context of gestures, postures, corporate actions, and song is necessary to give specific reference and focus to the stories, images, and experiences of distinctively Christian worship.

In our time, all reforms among a broad spectrum of Christian families must come to terms with the relationships between word and action. All of us are now exploring what the biblical witness and the early Church tradition took for granted: the worship of God is essentially the gathered community in active remembering, proclaiming, confessing, self-giving, and supplication in response to and in dialogue with God. This gathered body is called to present itself before God and to offer its sacrifice of praise and thanksgiving in such a manner as to become the time and place of epiphany, a living symbol to the world of the world remembered and redeemed.

31

Faithful liturgy discloses God's life with us so far as it has the power to open up levels of human being to ourselves and to God. Yet authentic worship also veils God from us, lest our prayer presume to contain God in its words or control the divine presence in worship. Above all, we now wish to affirm that authentic worship enacts the mystery of faith in the very signs God has given us: water, bread, wine, oil, fire, the laying on and lifting up of hands, utterance, and the graced rhythm of gathering and scattering.

If we are to understand symbol in liturgy, we must first understand that verbal texts have range and reference and emotional power to speak the mysteries of faith, insofar as they grow out of and lead back to that which is beyond the words. Having the right words in the right order, accompanied by the right gestures and supportive music, is not enough. Life must be brought to the words and acts. Participation in the hidden languages of time and space of sound and sight, of taste, texture, and bodily movement, is an essential condition for the human words to be come God's living Word to us and for the signs employed to become living symbols. Merely to use the signs and the words to assist in some individualist act of personal reminiscence or recalled felt experience is not sufficient. Private devotion cannot be substituted for participation in the life-giving corporate memories enacted in the Church's rites. Yet the interior life is necessary to discern and appropriate what is present in the signs enacted, the stories told, and the commands to act in daily life.

We will return to this point at length. For now, suffice it to say that these hidden languages enable us to experience an emotional intensity that transforms what we speak and what we do with the signs. So the quality of love, care, and hospitality at eucharist or in a foot washing, for example, creates powerful silences and spaces for discernment. The loving gesture "speaks," but faithful and attentive participation in these languages themselves depends upon commitment to the realities symbolized. Only by discernment and growing participation in those forms of communication that use the texts and signs can the assembled believers move beyond conventional faith, all too comfortably expressed in buttoned-down and perfunctory styles of "doing the liturgy."

That signs may become living symbols in our liturgy: this is our hope and prayer. Why is this so? Recall again the various things symbolized in the rites of initiation: cleansing, incorporation, anointing, illuminating, dying and rising, empowering — all given in the human words and natural signs of water, oil, the laying on of hands, words spoken, light, and food and all taking us into the reality signified. But note that such words and signs have power to symbolize and to carry us over to a new reality precisely as they bring us to disorientation and reorientation in our emotions and passions. The patterns of our desire and the very objects of regard and affection are re-oriented — that is, in our experienced participation. Symbols thus open up reality in the very process of opening up dimensions of the soul and the community's shared experience of the gospel mystery. Our emotions and deep affections are necessarily involved because a living symbol brings together the other and the self in a crucible of ordered ambiguity in our experience. The ambiguity is not confusion or disorder; rather, it is richness or experienced meaning that holds opposites in tension: dying to self and yet alive to God, renunciation yet fullness of being, remaining in this world yet citizen of another, and so on. Thus the waters of baptism, or the meal of eucharist, or the lights of eventide in our daily prayer all mean more than can be understood in one praying, much less said in one explanation.

Talk about symbol and the symbols of faith can be misleading. We have inherited a one-sided tradition which has regarded symbols as "things" that somehow contain power, or at least cause grace to be transmitted. No one here wishes to deny that the signs of water, bread, wine, and oil are related to God's grace. The question is not so much with the "what" of the signs causing grace as with the "how" of signs becoming living symbols.

Our concern is with how signs in the context of prayer and ritual action become focal points of the encounter between the human and the divine. The "how" is related to their use by a community which has a history and which is unafraid of its own experienced world. It is this having a history in remembering, and opening up the interior life to God, which governs and releases the emotional and cognitive range of the signs-become-symbols. Symbols are decidedly not things. Rather, they are crucibles of experience and places of epiphany.

Participation in religious symbol thus depends on our capacities to live into a particular history and into our own lives, both in relation to others and within its interior regions. Only by attending to the processes of lived history and human experience can we begin to understand how the question of presence, divine and human, is linked to the nonverbal dimensions of symbol and symbolization in liturgy. Regis Duffy, in a provocative essay entitled "Of Reluctant Celebrants and Reliable Symbols," writes, "Redemptive symbol, liturgically celebrated, can evoke our responsible presence. But this depends ... on an increasing ability to deal with our lived experience" (p. 173).

Symbols can never guarantee presence, either human or divine. That is because symbols are not things to be manipulated. Rather, if symbols are anything, we may describe them as crucibles of experience and meaning that occur in the context of narrative enacted. Thus symbolism must never be confused with ceremonial ornamentation of meanings already understood. Symbolic interaction of people in a context of ritual communication is itself generative. This is precisely why we can never exhaust primary symbols of faith: the cross encountered in the liturgy of Holy Week always disrupts our normal relation to doctrinal understanding and to our own self-awareness before God. Acknowledging that we have faith in the Crucified One can never be faithfully done as a matter of objective belief in a symbol. The faith itself is formed and expressed in the encounter with the Crucified One — in the liturgical gestures and actions, within the narrative of Christ's life witnessed in Scripture and proclamation, in our going to meet him in his coming to meet us. We can not simply make symbols by manipulating objects.

But the symbolizing of encounter with God is given in the signs and sign-actions handed down to us with our evangelization into a community of prayer. The issue of more faithful liturgy is thus a matter of more adequate evangelization into the narrative and into the form and style of life that enacts the narrative. This is much more than saying that word and rite must interact, or that the verbal and nonverbal aspects of symbol must be related. The question facing us is conversion into the very capacities required for participation in the symbolized encounter and ongoing life with God. Such conversion and commitment involves bringing our own social and interior experience to the remembered and enacted history. This involves a human subjectivity formed in the capacity to respond. Symbols without human subjectivity (passionate relatedness) will be empty; human faith without the symbols of liturgical action will be blind.

This is what Joseph Gelineau in *The Liturgy Today and Tomorrow* meant in his observation (pp. 98 - 99):

> Only if we come to the liturgy without hopes or fears, without longings or hunger, will the rite symbolize nothing and remain an indifferent or curious "object." Moreover, people who are not accustomed to poetic, artistic, or musical language or symbolic acts among their means of expression and communication find the liturgy like a foreign country whose customs and language are strange to them.

Thus far we have been exploring the nature of symbol as an interactive and generative feature of Christian liturgy. Let us turn to the main thesis promised at the beginning of this chapter. First, however, let me make explicit what has perhaps only been implicit to this point. We have noted all along that twentieth-century reforms and pastoral work or renewal of worship have rediscovered and reasserted a fundamental claim about the action character of liturgy. Any meaningful discussion of the sacraments must be in the context of liturgical prayer. We have, in short, reclaimed the ancient truth: worship is fundamentally the responsive gesture of the people of God. Furthermore, signs and words and images have power and range to mediate the reality and presence of God when human subjectivity is brought to them in forms appropriate to the activities of remembering, thanking, and supplicating God.

Suppose that we go on to give this abstract definition of a Christological focus: Christian liturgy is the ongoing word and prayer action of Jesus Christ in and through his body in the world. Here the characteristics of worship in sign, word, and image become focused and given content by the pattern of worship and life we discern in him: teaching, preaching, touching, healing, reconciling, feeding, suffering, obedience unto death, and being raised to new life. The whole history of God with the world and with the people God has called forth to covenant faith is brought to symbolic and ritual focus in the liturgy of Jesus Christ. So far as we recognize and accept ourselves as baptized into his life and death and resurrected presence, we become participants in this ongoing Word and prayer action. This indeed is his continuing life in our midst; but it is also to become our own "sacrifice of praise and thanksgiving." Not only are we to do these things (and speak these things) in remembering him, but we must learn how to offer ourselves in union with him. So our prayer and our lives are finally to be the continuous web of praise, thanksgiving, and self-offering to God whom Jesus calls Father.

Christian liturgy, in its whole economy (rites of initiation, eucharist, the daily prayer, the cycles of time, and the range of sacramental life) is response to God in creation, in time and history, in prophecy and precept, in care for neighbor and for the very created order itself. The world itself is thus potentially symbolic of God. And what we abstractly call the Paschal mystery is the storm center, the crux of such a vision of the world. The various ranges of symbol, primary and secondary, are understood only so far as we live with Jesus Christ over time. Understanding and being grasped by the nonverbal dimension of the primary symbols is thus a way of living out the baptismal grace and covenant that authentic conversion, prophetic Word, and sacramental life imply.

All this, of course, opens up new awareness of the hidden languages beyond the words we speak and hear and the signs we enact in the various liturgical actions of the Church. Living with the symbols itself takes time, place, audibility, visibility, and tangibility. Only with a deepening awareness of how these non-verbal languages release the experiential range of symbol can we begin to allow the symbols to symbolize the reality and mystery of faith for us.

Time

First, the non-verbal language of time. The significance of eating and drinking together takes time. This is why, in everyday life, we come to understand only after we have had meals on birthdays, anniversaries, after funerals, with all the children home and with them gone, and in all the subtly changing seasons of our lives in ordinary circumstances. It takes time in our eating together, in seasons of intensity and in seasons of leisure, to awaken us to all that these gestures mean. The point is obvious with respect, then, to Christian liturgy, and not only to the eucharistic meal. Symbols deepen as we mature with them. This is the secret of their nonverbal inexhaustibility.

So the language of time involves the discipline of the cycles of days, weeks, and years. Time is essential to remembering who God is and what God has done and to mark the particularity of what God promises to do in the signs and actions and words given to the Church. The Jewish cycles of time, with feasts and seasons, were carried over as a kind of depth grammar into the Christian patterns of liturgy in the first centuries of the Church. But because the primary symbols of eating and drinking — the laying on of hands, the reading from the book, and so on — are forever fused with the liturgy of Jesus (his life and work; suffering, death, and resurrection), our liturgical times are given focus and anchorage in a whole history. So the liturgical year is itself a Christological treasury of our corporate memories of who God in Christ is: his advent and birth, his appearance and ministry, his life and teaching, his passion, suffering, and death, his resurrection, ascension, and giving of life of Spirit to his people. Within this disciplined praxis of time we live with the signs, words, acts, and gestures becoming symbol. For it takes time to remember and trace out what connections these matters have with our lives, our social relatedness, our vision and existence in the world before God.

Space

The second non-verbal language that serves to give existential pathos to the symbols in liturgy is place. The places in which we gather and the uses of the spaces involved have a profound effect upon the quality and point of liturgical action. Certain spaces invite a static and sedentary approach to God — for example, an auditorium for hearing. Other spaces invite movement, freedom of encounter and gesture, uncluttered contemplation, and visual focus and provide significant acoustical images for hearing and singing. There are at least two dimensions of how the language of place and space affects our understanding and life with symbol.

On the one hand, in a local parish community there is the embodied history of the building and the interior spaces where families have gathered for generations; where weddings, funerals, and all other rites of passage have taken place, where eucharist has been received, and the sound of prayer has given association to the action itself. The sense of local history of prayer and life is part of the hidden language of place, which all must respect. We who worship God in a particular building are shaped by the place and its history (or lack thereof!).

But there is also the arrangement of the space as environment for symbolization, for the environment itself symbolizes our sense of God and human relatedness in liturgy. How we arrange furnishings — altar table, reading stand, place of preaching, font, seats, place of music — determines what is heard and seen. But it also expresses what we believe about the relationships between words spoken and the sacramental sign-acts, between prayer and human encounter, faith and action.

Sound and Silence

A third language is that of sound and silence. Music is but the extension of speech. The silences between words are as important as the sounds themselves, for both together create the primary acoustical image with which we pray. Music and silence must surround the reading and hearing of the Church's corporate memories contained in the Scriptures. The art forms of music — congregational, choral, and instrumental — grow naturally out of this fundamental perception. Singing is an extension of speaking; music is the language of the soul becoming audible.

But just as the music requires much attention to the spaces between notes, so our worship must learn once again to attend to our need for silence. The spaces surrounding our words must be deep and honest. Here we can learn something from the Quaker tradition. In a culture wich bombards us with sound wherever we go, the practice of quiet is healing. Worship which is alive and "active" may miss the fact that we need to recollect and receive by listening in active silence in order to hear God. The use of music in worship should never be mere ornamentation of the Word but rather its expression. There is a hidden music in how we dance (gather and scatter, stand and sit, move and come to stillness) and how we speak that which music should serve to express.

The Visual Gesture and Movement

Fourth, the language of sign and symbol leads us directly to the question of how we celebrate the visible, tactile, and kinetic language in the sacramental actions of the gospel, most especially baptism and the Lord's Supper. I must confine myself here to one observation: uncovering the depth language of the gestures of taking, blessing, breaking, and sharing is absolutely essential to our Christian life. Likewise, learning to celebrate the mystery of dying and rising with the whole congregation, rather than tacking on a convenient little ceremony with the baby, is of utmost importance to our recovery of the powerful beauty of conversion and initiation in faith and the release of its symbolism in our lives over time. We will return to remembering baptism in Chapter Four and to the language of the fourfold action at the Lord's table in Chapter Five.

The words we use in singing, praying, listening and responding do not stand alone. They depend upon symbol and the range of nonverbal languages for depth and point. What we see with our eyes, how we gesture and move — these intensify and give personal, sensory focus to the stories and images we speak and hear. Stories, prophecies, and teachings are interwoven with acts such as seeing the flame of the Paschal candle, reaching to receive bread, passing the peace, standing to sing, moving to and from spaces around the table, the font and the place of the Word. Because of this interweaving, the worshiping assembly comes to behold what earthly eyes have not yet seen, nor ears yet heard. The words speak mystery and grace this way.

The fusion of word with what is seen and gestured is powerfully expressed by Gail Ramshaw and Linda Ekstrom in the series, *Words Around the Fire. . .The Table. . .The Font*: "In the assembly we are flown by God into light and health and justice, for we are carried by the Spirit into the outstretched arms of Christ." (*Words Around the Table,* p. 7)

We see, then, how crucial is the awakening and sustaining of a capacity to respond to symbols. In considering the hidden languages, we have also touched upon specific directions for catechesis and faith formation. This brings us to the most critical agenda: restoring a sense of history to the symbols and the ritual action. This can never be done by teaching theory or even good doctrine alone. It must be evocative, imaginative, and experiential — but consistently grounded in the biblical witness to a living faith community. Of equal importance to faith formation is the restoration of the Church's self-corrective memory of God's history with us and the overcoming of our being strangers to our own experience of life (fear and hope, suffering and death, guilt and forgiveness, reconciliation and joy).

This agenda should remind us that we never have easy access to the "pure" archetypal meaning of symbols. The cross reveals and conceals, the water bath also, as does ongoing word (read, preached, prayed, sung) and the eating and drinking of the eucharistic meal. The mode of participation in the primary symbols of faith is necessarily cultural. Whatever we may wish to say about the multivalency of water and the rites of initiation, or of bread and wine in the context of eucharistic memorial, or of light in the context of vespers or the Easter vigil, any particular liturgical celebration employing such signs is always influenced by the social reality and expectations of particular communities of faith. Liturgy is something done by real women and men in real times and places.

In other words, the tacit range of meaning available is always selected out by the living hermeneutic of the worshiping assembly and given emotional focus in the societal perceptions and orientations we have been invited to bring. So it is, for example, that in our age the eucharistic bread presents us with a prophetic icon of a hungry world alongside its significance as "presence" and "bread from heaven." Thus we may be able to regain in our time a heightened discernment of the primary symbolism of meal or banquet. Augustine's exegesis of the bread asked for in the Lord's Prayer may suddenly ring true (as it may not have in an earlier time): we ask for daily bread and for the eschatological bread, and these are mutually sustaining. Bread for the hungry world, in which we are called to responsibility, and the bread of the Realm have much to do with each other. And this does not reduce the meaning of the bread symbolism; rather, it enriches and renders more powerful our own mystery, which we receive from God in the eucharist. Hasten the day when all shall gather at such a table.

But think also of the suppressed symbolism of the sacrificial ritual that includes the sign of bread: violence and death. To observe this aspect of the whole eucharistic action is not, of course, to claim that the real meaning behind the images of sacrifice is violence. Rather, it shows how dense and deeply intertwining the strands of the symbolism are. Thus a powerful reading, or a sermon, or a prayer of intercession, or a piece of music deeply heard may shock us into the imaginative and real awareness of this suppressed symbolism in the whole pattern of eucharist. Our own world comes into focus precisely at this table; we can never domesticate it. But neither can we separate the cultic and the ethical dimensions of what we do here!

The primary hidden language of symbol is, of course, the human body and its life in community. Jesus' own liturgy finally involved his laying down his life and stretching out his arms on the cross for us and for all the world. In that strange and terrifying manner he was glorified; and it is his risen life, still manifesting the human marks of

41

suffering love, that animates the Church as his body in the world here and now. It is by virtue of the extension of this meaning that we may once again speak of the gathered assembly as the basic symbol. We can only participate in this so far as we learn its hidden languages.

Alexander Schmemann, in addressing the topic of the organic unity of liturgy and the sacrament of Christ, urges upon us that the essential function of living liturgy is, and has always been, "to bring together, within one symbol, the three levels of the Christian faith and life: the Church, the world, and the Kingdom." It is finally only here — in the *mysterion* of God's presence and action — that the Church may become what it is: The Body of Christ and the Temple of the Holy Spirit, "the unique Symbol, 'bringing together,' by bringing to God the world for the life of which God gave his only son" (p. 105).

One more thing must be said. We have been speaking of the meaning and point of the nonverbal aspects of symbol in the liturgy from a human point of view, attempting to throw some light on the patterns of experience and the capacities for response that are conditions for sacramental/liturgical life. True worship is that continual occasioning through time of the divine-human dialogue, the ongoing prayer of Christ in his people animated by the Holy Spirit. The central mystery of Christian life and worship is found here: Christ prays in the world for the world, in and through our prayers in his name. And in the symbols that convey the reality and power of death and resurrection, our worship draws us into the very life of God — now and in God's ultimate Reign to come.

Four

Living Baptism

Therefore we have been buried with him by baptism into death, so that, just as Christ was raised from the dead by the glory of the Father, so we too might walk in newness of life.

ROMANS 6:4

At the heart of the Christian faith is our participation in the dying and rising of Jesus Christ and our being drawn into the triune life of God. This participation is itself the essence of every faithful gathering for worship. In every liturgy of Word and Sacrament we are reoriented toward this life in the Spirit. Such a participation involves conversion and growth in grace toward the fullness of who Jesus Christ is. To participate is thus to remember our baptism and be thankful. But it is, as we noted in Chapter One, to remember that we are adopted sons and daughters — engrafted onto the living history of God's people. "Memory believes before knowledge remembers."

All that the Creator of heaven and earth has accomplished and brought to focus in the life, passion, death and resurrection, and the living intercession of Jesus Christ for all humanity is now and always present to the gathered community. The baptismal creed is a narrative of God for us, creating, redeeming, and bringing to completion God's beloved. God's future for humanity, even for the entire cosmos, is present yet anticipated in this unfathomable and unmerited gift by "water and the Spirit." Baptism is God initiating in us God's eschatological gift. This is the final gift, the alpha and omega of our life. It is as though God were to say to each of us, "I was your beginning, I walked with you on your journey, and now I await you as your homecoming."

43

Living out the baptized life is our theme. Becoming the persons God calls us to be is a lifelong process of turning and returning to God. The new creation itself must grow into the holiness conferred. Baptism initiates the double journey into our own humanity and into life with God. Baptismal spirituality therefore requires our humanity at full stretch in relation to God and to the whole human community. In this way, baptism into Jesus' dying and rising is the charter for all ministry in his name. From God's own womb we are born. Into the stature and fullness of Christ we must grow.

One of the most difficult facts of our existence is that it takes appreciation. The loss of the familiar and the comfortable surroundings of friends and family may occasion new depth and new maturity. In the midst of the old and the dying, the new comes to birth. These facts help explain why Jesus uses the image of the seed, which, sown into the earth, must die as seed in order to live as grain. Growth in Christian understanding of self and the world requires this awareness.

If awareness of the relation between the death of the old and the life that springs forth is true of the natural world and of our own inner life, how much more is this true of the way of God with us. We long to be delivered from those ancient powers that hold the natural and the historical world captive. The bondage of sin, death, and corruption is real. We can avoid these matters just so long. Soon or late the cry rises within us, "Set us free!" Without some sense of being held captive, it is exceedingly difficult for us to understand what being delivered might be. Fate, sin, guilt, the corruptibility of the flesh, and the malleability of our wills — these are elemental features highlighted by the whole sweep of Scripture. These are the realities that fix our interest and hold us captive.

The gospel claims that baptism into Christ's death and resurrection brings deliverance from such powers. Can we say we are "born anew," born by dying — by burial? No wonder this is too much for us! The bondage is sometimes only seen after a long time. Sometimes the deliverance is conferred before we can be fully aware of the powers that hold us from life and from our own best being.

44

The unfolding of what is given in baptism must therefore take a lifetime — and it does. This is what we mean in asserting that the Church confesses its baptism every time we gather in the name of God under the Word and signs of faith's mystery. Whether in a small rural church with a few, or in the heart of a cathedral in a great city, the Church manifests by its very gathering that our lives are hid with Christ in God. Those who are familiar with suffering and death in their own lives and history are more open to the reality and power toward which the baptismal actions point.

"By water and the Holy Spirit [you have] made us a new people in Jesus Christ our Lord, to show forth [your] glory in all the world," reads the third proper preface from the eucharistic prayer in the *Book of Common Prayer*. Being made new by dying to the old is what God intends for us and for all the world. The image of the new creation applies not only to individuals but to the entire created order. Baptism is, in this way, a metaphor for the continuing whole work of God in the cosmos.

How do we embrace these astounding matters? Recall the phrase that occurs in the letter to the church at Ephesus: "One Lord, one faith, one baptism" (4:5). With these words, the early community of faith and all of us are called to rediscover our true identity and unity in Jesus Christ crucified and risen. This is not a unity with the pious, or even with all who confess the faith. It is a unity with all of the created and historical orders yearning for newness in God.

The meaning and import of Christian initiation (baptism and/or confirmation) has come to center stage during the past few years. The relationship between how we actually celebrate baptism and the kind and quality of living faith is no longer a matter for the clergy alone. Laypersons too are concerned with recovering the whole structure of Christian conversion and initiation.

This is because when our baptismal understandings are weak, our understanding of the nature and character of the entire Christian life is weak. Issues concerning baptism and the whole pattern of initiation into the community of faith have been made prominent by three basic facts: (1) the ecumenical movement and the growing need to recognize our basic unity in Christ, stimulated most recently by the Second Vatican Council; (2) the extraordinary fruits of historical scholarship, which has revealed the early Church and the Reformation sources that give us a sense of the converging structures of the baptismal rites; and (3) the emerging global religious situation, which has forced Christians to raise basic questions about our identity, each in an individual cultural and social context. Cultural diversity among Christians generates questions concerning our claims about God, Jesus, the nature of sin, and the nature of salvation. In light of these factors we will explore the image of a "new creation through water and the Spirit."

Baptismal Remembering

What does it mean for us to "Remember your baptism and be thankful," as the United Methodist service of baptismal renewal proclaims? It is related to the shaping, guiding, and praying hard work of the common life of the Church. We cannot renew the sense of baptismal life by writing new theologies of baptism. The reform of the patterns and the texts used is necessary, but the renewal of our capacities to enter into and participate in the baptismal covenant and reaffirmation of faith is beyond the texts and the words. It involves solidarity with the suffering ones.

We do not have to work very long with local churches to discover our unease and underlying lack of clarity about baptism. Simply observe the way we typically celebrate — or fail to celebrate — baptisms and confirmations. The key words are so often "convenience," "without lengthy instruction," "tacked on," and the like. Our characteristic approach to the celebration of baptism is uninformed and uninspired. Laity and clergy have simply not received sound teaching. When is the last time you heard a profound baptismal sermon or attended a class of inquirers in which the laity assisted the pastor(s) in forming the faith of those seeking baptism and/or confirmation? We must confess our faults. We have not given or been allowed the opportunity to experience the renewal of our own baptismal life. Until recently, it has been something of a scandal in seminaries that teaching of the sacraments has been impoverished.

Of course, in such a situation, misunderstandings abound. Consider the following. Recently, several local pastors told me that they have been rebaptizing certain persons. They told me point-blank that they rebaptized people who so requested it because they now claim a "true conversion." Many persons told of how they could not remember anything about their baptism or christening as infants or young children. Since they could not associate in their conscious remembrance any "experience" of Christ, but had now had a dramatic moment or event of encounter with Christ, the earlier baptism was obviously not valid or, as some reported, "It must not have taken."

Apart from the fact that the idea of baptism as an inoculation seems a bit odd, we have here a pastoral reality that calls into question the integrity of what was done in the name of God. This book cannot untangle the problems of what constitutes a "valid" in contrast to an "invalid" sacramental action of the Church. What commands our attention is the relationship between the action of the gathered Church at the baptismal font — whether involving an infant or an adult, whether by full immersion or by pouring or sprinkling — and specific experiences of encounter with Jesus Christ. Baptismal spirituality does not depend upon one particular sequence of conscious experience and the covenant implied in the baptismal action of the Church. In fact, it is necessary that there be many relationships over time between the specific ritual action of the gathered Church and various kinds of experiences, both dramatic and ordinary.

To remember our baptism is not primarily a matter of recalling a consciously experienced dramatic event. Such a consciously recalled "converting experience" may be a crucial part of the history of the baptized person's life, but it is only one moment in a whole process. Some Christian traditions have held that one must first consciously experience and witness to saving faith before the baptismal action of the Church is administered. Others have emphasized that the baptismal action with water and in the name of God with the laying on of hands (and anointing) will elicit a specific faith response over time. The latter view assumes a faithful church whose members support, nourish, and sustain a lively sense of the dying and rising with Christ as the environment into which infants may grow until, as more mature persons, they come to profess their own faith and experience. In the case of persons whose baptism is preceded by strong converting experiences, the rites have a more direct expressive power and witness to the faith professed by the individual and the Church together.

In all cases of genuine baptismal life in Christ, however, to remember our baptism is a matter of recognition of all that God has done and is yet to do in our lives. Remembering moments of great crisis, submission, and "blessed assurance" is a significant part of the community's history — as well as of each believer's history and identity. But recognition of the saving mystery beyond our conscious personal experiences is also necessary. Remembering specific experiences is itself dependent upon the unfolding mystery of our life in Christ. Saving faith takes the time and space of a whole lifetime and requires a faithful community in which to continually renew that faith, along with its multiple experiences. So in any renewal or reaffirmation of the baptismal grace of God — particularly at confirmation, for those faithfully baptized as infants, and especially for the whole church each Easter or other festal time of renewal — is to recognize the funded experience of the people of God in all times and places!

Becoming Who We Are

This leads us to the heart of Christian spirituality: becoming who we already are in Christ. The meanings of baptism are many, but one that bears directly upon the inherited memories of the whole people of God is "adoption." In baptism we are made new in Christ and adopted heirs of the promises of God given from the beginning of God's relation with creation and with a people called out. We are engrafted into the history of Israel and thus must come to terms with a history not ours. We must grow into our inheritance. The root metaphor of adopted sons and daughters bears considerable reflection. For if we are in baptism thus incorporated into a living history of covenant and suffering and search and saving faith, we must come to share in our new family's history. We can only share the stories and the remembered narratives as our own by recognizing that God has given us a history and a name. Once we had no name; now we have a name — we are become a "royal priesthood." Baptism is the conferral of a name and a promise and a history to be discovered and made our own, but always in our specific time and place, with our specific cultural and historical memories. Any claims to pedigree and pride and place can never be a right. We have the treasure of God's gift only by God's gracious act in Christ.

The relationships between the baptismal liturgy of the Church and the experiences of the converted life are many and complex. If we think of baptism primarily as God's enacted promise to be faithful to us throughout our whole lifetimes, just as God's covenant with the world is one of steadfast love forever, then specific experiences of renewed conversion ought to be celebrated as part of the ongoing life of the community of faith. But powerful new experiences of Christ, even when they seem to be so radical, do not warrant rebaptism. Rather, they call for joyful thanksgiving and renewal on our part. Christian faith claims that God is always at work in our lives, even when we are unaware and do not acknowledge it.

I have been moved deeply by the public testimony of persons who have chosen to reaffirm their baptismal vows because they have come to new levels of discernment concerning the hidden work of grace. Many laypersons have spoken of a whole new understanding of lifelong baptismal grace because they have undertaken the recovery of Lenten discipline as a time of spiritual preparation for the renewal of their own baptismal covenant along with the newly baptized and confirmed at Easter or at Pentecost. When the whole community of believers undertakes an intentional recovery of Lent, Holy Week, and Easter-Pentecost as a special time of intensive participation in the reality of Christ's dying and rising, the opportunities for deeper converting experiences are greater. For this language of liturgical time has been associated since the beginning of Christianity with the rites of initiation into the body of the faithful.

This leads us to a fundamental proposal: the whole process and structure of Christian initiation must be recovered and given primary attention by local churches. We must find a way to create a more receptive environment for the whole Church's disciplined approach to every baptism, or at least to the Lent-Easter time as a season of baptismal renewal. Faithfully to embody our "new creation" in Christ demands such a disciplined spirituality. If we are to experience, celebrate, and faithfully live out our new life in Christ, the process and structure of baptism and confirmation and their inner connection with every eucharist must be recovered for the whole Church. The "new creation" is liturgically centered in the baptismal vocation to be a servant Church — to the particular ministries in the world God will give us. Such a recovered discipline and vision should combine evangelical and catholic impulses and render these practical in our time and place.

To remember our baptism, then, is to recognize God's initiative and the sovereignty of God's rule and righteousness and love. Despite the resistances born of lack of understanding, many American Protestant traditions, as well as Roman Catholic ones, are beginning to stress the discipline of baptismal practice and spirituality. How can we communicate the fullness of God's gift in baptism unless we claim boldly that the very act of baptizing into Christ is a future-orienting and identity-conferring covenant with God? Baptism sets up a wide range of explicit and implicit possibilities for human existence. Sins are forgiven — so how shall we live with one another? We are incorporated into Christ's body on earth — so how can we show that we belong to him? We have union with Jesus' work— so how can we be Christ for a broken and starving and death-bent world? We have received the gift of the Holy Spirit — so how shall those gifts for ministry and all fruits of the Spirit be manifest in our lives? We have been born anew — so how shall we grow toward maturity and into the full stature of the humanity of Christ?

We can now begin to see that baptism into Christ is far more than celestial fire insurance. It is far more than a ritual act of cleansing with water in the name of the triune God. It is far more than our own act of self-surrender and faithful commitment following upon a religious experience. It may be all of these. The New Testament, and Paul in particular, uses the expression "in Christ" to refer to a whole pattern of intentions, dispositions, and actions in which the grace of Christ becomes manifest in our own existence. Our living theology depends radically upon the depth of prayer, biblical understanding, mutuality in love, and vulnerability in service to the world. The gifts and graces of the Holy Spirit conferred in baptism are nothing if they are not shared and lived in concrete human relations. All of these are hidden as the promised future in baptism.

For baptism has both a narrow and a comprehensive meaning for us. The water bath in the name of God with the laying on of hands is the narrow meaning. It refers to that specific moment or rite. In this sense it is always subject to criticism as a "mere" empty ceremonial activity of the Church. The "real" faith experience may be elsewhere, according to some traditions of piety. And, of course, without recovered discipline and understanding, a practice such as infant baptism can become indiscriminate and even misleading.

Yet baptism also refers to the whole inexhaustible meaning of incorporation into the dynamic and continuing reality of Christ, empowerment as his body in the world, and into the life of faith, which must constantly struggle and grow in grace. The texts and sign actions of the Church in baptism and confirmation should not and cannot be abstracted from the matrix of faith. The whole life of the Church is at stake. Baptism is at once a specific sacramental act of the Church and an ongoing process of becoming disciples of Christ. Both the Church's actions and God's gracious activity are involved. But the faith experience of believers and the recognition of God's powerfully hidden ways with us are involved too. One cannot be without the other. Augustine's aphorism is right to the point: "Without God, we cannot. Without us, God will not." Let us turn to what it is "in us" that the Holy Spirit and grace in baptism works upon over our lifetime.

Images of Life Experience

Baptism cannot be understood apart from the patterns of experience, affection, passion, desire, and intention that are the regenerative features of the Christian life. It is not enough simply to believe that Christ died for our sins. Baptism is never a mere act of assent, any more than it is a matter of one "proper" or "valid" ceremonial tradition. The whole body of the Church must share the experience of being baptized — both with those who are evangelized and in the life of mutual service and love to the community beyond the Church. The experience of God's saving grace will never be real and powerful until our concrete social relationships are transformed. To be heirs of the promises of God is to belong to God's work in the world.

This drives us to a new point of understanding. We must first recover the living images of baptism from the New Testament and the whole tradition. Then we must find the most adequate and powerful ways to render those images in our celebrations and teachings. The very structure of the catechumenate, or training period for converted life and Church membership, should reflect those primary images. Finally, we must become living images of Christ. Only this way, by immersing ourselves in the living images of God's grace and by trusting the symbolic depth beyond our conscious awareness of the sign-actions of baptism and confirmation, can we begin to address the deficiencies in baptismal theology and spirituality we have all inherited in the American churches.

Think again of the biblical images: participation in Christ's dying and rising; new birth, washing and cleansing from sin, renewal and illumination by the Holy Spirit, anointing to ministry. Yet there is more, born from the whole history of God's people and burned into the memory of the Church: exodus from slavery, liberation to a new land and way of life, salvation from chaos, delivery from the Flood. Still more: reclothing in Christ, new garments, solidarity in the Church, unity and love, putting on the whole armor of God. "Which does baptism really mean?" ask the literal-minded and the skeptical alike.

The gospel says in reply, "Baptism means all these images, and more!" The multivalency of meanings resides in the images that are given in God's revelation and reside in the faithful lives of the saints. Who are the saints? Not the super-pious, the religious heroes and heroines; not, certainly, the religiously successful. The saints are those baptized who struggle to live life in light of God's faithful promises. The saints are those whose holiness is ordinary but whose identity is extraordinary. For their identity is found in humble service and in the redemptive marks of love in the hands of God — the nail-scarred hands of Jesus of Nazareth.

The early Church patterns show forth a process in which baptism is not isolated but rather embedded in the midst of the community's own ongoing faith and life. This is why the martyrs, it is said, were "baptized in their own blood." But there were countless numbers of nonmartyrs who participated in the same saving reality of the water and blood that flowed from the side of Christ. Only by learning to live again by the baptismal images of the New Testament, and by the images and symbols given in the whole history of God's people into which we are adopted in Christ, can we find life together.

There is, of course, an ambiguity in our appeal to experience. On the one hand we tend to think of "an experience" of God's grace as an episode — of joy, relief from guilt, peace, the feeling of being born and supported. This is often an intensely felt emotion and complex of feelings.

Baptism is related to such particular experiences — but not in some simple chronological manner. Still, many church-goers lack such experiences of the heart and hence have never discerned the power of baptismal grace. Faith completely devoid of emotional experience of this sort is only of the head, not of the heart.

But there is another notion of experience in relation to living out our baptism that is crucial. We speak of experience not as a feeling but as a whole pattern of life come to intensity — a basic attunement to the deepest reality. Experience in this sense is an affective relatedness to life over a period of time. The whole of one's life may be said to be an experience of grace, whether the dark night of the desert way or intimacy with God. We need to recover the sense of baptismal experience that refers to the whole of our life wherein certain emotions and dispositions are central.

Think of the baptized life as one in which Paul can command certain deep emotions: "Rejoice in the Lord always"; "Give thanks in all circumstances"; "Remember your baptism and be thankful." Here the focus is upon emotions that characterize a life received from God.

So we must speak of baptismal experience in both ways. There are specific times of intense feeling and particular points of repentance, release from guilt, sudden and overwhelming assurance, convicting sense of God's presence. At the same time, living out our baptism into Christ means the manifestation of long-term passions for God and neighbor. Our love for God may itself have its ups and downs, fits and starts. But God's love for us is not dependent upon the ups and downs and fits and starts of human interiority. One of the ironies of pietist traditions may be not that we have stressed experience too much but that we have not stressed the deeper meaning of experience enough!

The point, of course, is conversion to God. The depth of conversion is precisely a deepening life of experienced relationship with God and discipleship in love and service to neighbor. That is what the whole process of initiation into Christ's body signifies. In order for our baptismal rites to show more of the reality and power of the biblical witness, the level of maturity of faith in the whole community must be addressed. We have settled for too little. In defining conversion as felt emotion, part of our tradition has turned away from the long-range deep emotions that constitute the very life of faith with God. The promises of God's Word and the process of turning and returning again to the source of our life in Christ are the font and the summit of all experience of the Spirit.

Who among us can tell when a fully mature response to God's free offer of grace has been made? The answer is: finally, none of us can presume. We are all journeying, we are all growing toward that which has been conferred by water and the Spirit. As our greatest teachers of prayer and the spiritual life remind us, we are all beginners, again and again. The most sustaining baptismal theology comes from those who have stressed God's sovereign love and initiative in Christ, and the notion of a continual sanctified life that is the journey.

Luther, in *The Babylonian Captivity of the Church,* claimed (p. 180), "The first thing to be considered about any baptism is divine promise which says who believes and is baptized is saved, for just as the truth of this divine promise once pronounced over us continues until our death, so our faith in it ought never to cease but to be nourished and strengthened until death by continually remembering the promise made to us in baptism." How do we remember this promise? By faithfully practicing the means of grace: Scripture, prayer, the Holy Supper, the discipline of fasting and almsgiving, speaking the truth in love and in serving the world with our whole compassion and skill.

Baptism is the sacrament of radical equality. For in Christ there "is neither Jew nor Greek, there is neither slave nor free, there is neither male nor female" (Gal. 3:28). This confers upon us a solidarity with all the wide earth and all those who dwell therein. For we are free of any need to assert our own claims, our own pedigree. The whole redemptive mystery of God is given in Christ, yet it needs the mystery of lives lived unto God to grasp its whole meaning.

The ground for our hope is that God's covenant with us — that intimacy between the mission of Jesus and the outpouring of the Spirit for service and life together — is forever. Nothing can separate us from this. The celebration of that self-giving of God to us is what we have yet to recover in fullness every time the community gathers at the font. God's continuing life, which is at one and the same time the outpouring of God toward the created order, is also moving back to God redeeming a broken and alienated world — reconciling it back to its source. In Jesus the world is won back, and in the Holy Spirit the animating breath of God seeks to renew the face of the earth. For us, this redemptive journey of God has its focal point in the cross and empty tomb. Our whole lives are called to express that in concrete redemptive ways. As struggling persons of faith, we have inadequacies to confess but unimaginable hope to profess. We have known so little of the spiritual witness to all this, yet have charisms to celebrate and to claim.

So we are called to be a community of remembrance and recognition in a world of perplexity and forgetfulness. We enact the symbols only to realize that it is Christ enacting them, in us, through us, and for us. "Remember your baptism and be thankful." Become who you are in God's embrace and sovereign love. But if baptism is the foundation and charter of our life in Christ, the eucharist is our sacrament for the journey. To that feast we turn.

Five

Take, Bless, Break, and Share

"It is your own mystery you receive...."

AUGUSTINE

Several years ago during the summer term at Notre Dame, a young priest from Kansas City drowned in Lake Michigan. Bob had been vibrant and life-loving. Just a few days earlier he had entertained the whole gathered community during the summer's mock initiation rites with his ingenious wit. We had been enjoying a delightful summer weekend when the news reached those back on campus. A student in my seminar had been with him that day, swimming in the choppy lake. One moment Bob was there, the next moment gone — pulled under the waves. The whole place was stunned. It was not possible. Unbelievable.

At the Requiem Mass in Sacred Heart Church we listened to the readings, remembered, heard a strong word, sang songs of faith with breaking voices, remembered and prayed and celebrated the mystery of the meal — the food taken and blessed, the bread broken and shared — and were brought painfully back to the essentials. I shall never forget the lines from the responsorial psalm that day:

> I sought the Lord, and he answered me, and delivered
> me out of all my terror....
> I called in my affliction, and the Lord heard me,
> and saved me from all my troubles....
> The angel of the Lord encompasses those who fear God
> and will deliver them.

(PSALM 34:4,7)

The point is not to stress our feelings of shock, grief, and sorrow, or even of thanksgiving for his life and ministry. These were real and felt, to be sure, and indelibly part of what will be suddenly called to mind in other times and places when we hear those words, sing those songs, and break the bread. The point is, in taking the fresh memory of that seemingly senseless death up into the remembering of the whole community and the whole Church in all times and places, our experiences were intensified and transfigured by the suffering and the mystery of God. Only by the conjoining of that real death with the memorial cried out in the acclamation "Christ has died, Christ is risen, Christ will come again!" could we begin to come to terms with what had happened. Thus Bob's memory is blessed to us because it is forever blessed in Christ and hid with him in God. The waters of death, the waters also of his and our baptisms, the light of Christ — all these were forever forged in the intensity of God's way with us in the Christian gospel.

None of us could — nor did we wish to — escape the fact of death, Bob's or our own. Yet we also knew in the profound simplicity of the gathering about the font, the book, and the table that, despite the contingencies of life and the pitch of grief, nothing could "separate us from the love of God in Christ Jesus" (Rom. 8:39). Such an experience of Christian worship shows the pattern of life, which can no longer be regarded as "mere ritual." The signs of gathering, singing, praying, and enacting the mystery of the holy meal become for us living symbols. Moreover, we find ourselves becoming persons marked with the reality those sign-actions signify, and we participate in what the symbols express.

If we are to have any sensible talk about Christian spirituality in our time, it must be refocused in the patterns of our common liturgy, and we must learn again to be reconfigured in the baptismal pattern and the fourfold action around the altar. Such a way of life, as I have suggested, cannot be understood or lived apart from the honest confrontation with suffering and mystery.

But most of the time human speech keeps us at a safe distance from the disorienting and painful features of our existence. Casual conversation fills us with pleasantry and passes the time of our days. Our very language stays with the dull, our humdrum complaints, our small vices, our petty expectations. This is simply who we are at small talk. The language of everyday life is characteristically without passion and imagination, save for a few turns of ornamental speech and the venting of frustration over the stupidity of others. Such is the semi-permanent forgetfulness of the essential matters. Such forgetfulness is part of the great deception in our contemporary culture. It commonly takes some tragic reminder to awaken us to some thing more than meets the eye and the ear. The liturgy waits for us. The sacrament of Christ's dying and rising remains waiting for us to bring our griefs and joys and most perplexing questions and heartfelt cries to the table.

Sacraments: Life-Sources

While there are varieties and types of Christian spirituality, all ways of living a godly life are, in the last analysis, sacramental. That is, our pattern of life is to be rooted in baptism and fed in the eucharist. Christians rightly confess "one Lord, one faith, one baptism." The whole of the Christian life is an unfolding in time and history of what is given in the whole gift of God in Christ. Participation in the reality and power of dying and rising to new life is the very heart of what it is to belong to Christ. "Remembering our baptism" is necessary to any mature faith, for coming to know and to understand ourselves as baptized persons takes time and grows by endurance of the tragic dimensions of life. Such coming to understand requires that our lives be made more and more open to suffering, to love, and to the range of emotions illuminated by the Holy Spirit. Whatever stage of life we may baptize, whether infants or adults, the crucial point is in the life lived out. The decisive fact is to live the ongoing life, in seasons and out, in daily routines as well as in anxiety, danger, suffering, and hope.

To live out the meaning of baptism propels us back to the sources of grace and courage. So, while there may be specific times of corporate reaffirmation and renewal of baptismal vows, every time we come to the table of the Lord we acknowledge and continue to grow into that which has been given by God "by water and the Spirit." To share the holy meal of the Lord's Supper presents us with a living Word, read and sung, prayed and proclaimed. Every work of mercy, each act of love, and all endeavors by the Church to serve the society in which we live are such reminders. But it is the eucharistic sharing that focuses most explicitly upon the manner in which the suffering of God may transform us.

When Augustine said to believers about the eucharist, "It is your own mystery you receive," he was not referring to a mere human interpretation of the ritual or to our personal religious consolations. Neither did he intend to say everything that needs to be said. Rather, Augustine focused upon the astonishing fact that we receive our identity and our own lives are transformed by the life-giving death and resurrection of Jesus. When we share the bread and the cup faithfully, it is precisely God's self-giving that conveys life to us. As Paul proclaims (I Cor. 10:16), "When we drink the cup, is it not a means of sharing in the blood of Christ? When we break the bread, is it not a means of sharing in the body of Christ?"

The meaning of these simple acts of sharing a meal can never be exhausted. In this sense the Lord's Supper is never a simple meal, for it bears our own mystery hid in God, and it prepares to take unto itself the whole world's suffering hope. We are invited to receive our own best being again and again, because all we have and are is from God alone. We did not make ourselves. At the same time, God has lavished love on the creatures and the whole creation, counting us worthy to stand and praise God and to receive our humanity in the ordinary means of food and drink. This is the work of human hands, which is all the more God's gracious hidden gift. The ordinary means of receiving God's offer of love is thus itself to be the pattern of our own lives together with God and with neighbor: offered, made holy, broken open, and lavished upon a hungry world.

In turning to the ancient, simple, yet inexhaustible pattern of how Christians are to give thanks and celebrate the meal, we turn to the ongoing sacrament of our life's journey. If baptism is our birth from the womb of God and the wellspring of new life from above, then the Lord's Supper is our manna for the way, our life-giving bread and saving cup. These are the living symbols in which God's own life and grace are offered in the midst of the world's travail and hope.

What We Do At Table

The four actions at the table — take, bless, break, and share — are what we are to become. Every Christian who remembers at the table recognizes a memory beyond her or his own conscious life history. Even in those traditions that have not celebrated the meal frequently we recognize the history into which we are adopted. The fourfold shape is derived from Jesus' meal with the disciples in which he uttered the unforgettable words, "This is my body." Faithfully explored, the pattern is far more than empty ritual. The pattern gives us the very shape of the life God calls us to live responsibly in this world.

It always comes as something of a shock to biblical fundamentalists to be reminded that the first generation of Christians evangelized, prayed, worshiped, and lived a disciplined life *before* the New Testament was written. The Scriptures grew out of the experiences and the living faith and a family of traditions, based in temple and synagogue, yet transformed by the death and resurrection of Christ. When we go to the New Testament for images of Christian worship and spirituality, we are already in the midst of living traditions of worship. Any understanding of the fourfold action depends on appreciating this fact from the outset. The Scriptures are themselves the fruit of a worshiping community; the celebration of the meal in Jesus' name gives meaning to the stories and memories that guided the very life of the community.

Paul reminds us in his account of the institution of the Lord's Supper (I Cor. 11:2-24) that "I received from the Lord what I also delivered to you, that the Lord Jesus on the night when he was betrayed took bread, and when he had given thanks, he broke it, and said, 'This is my body which is for you. Do this in remembrance of me.' "Or, more pointedly, "Do this as the re-experiencing of what I have done for you." Such a doing is the remembering in and through the meal. Life in accordance with the teaching of the apostles and in the continuing practice of the breaking of the bread, referred to in Acts 2:42ff., sustains the living memory of Jesus. What is said and done by the community gathered is embodied in the community scattered in word and deed.

Justin Martyr's *Apology*, written in the mid-second century but reflecting this same pattern of worship stretching back to the first evangelization of his little church at Rome, presents us with an extraordinary picture of the whole pattern of the Lord's Supper (p. 9):

> On the day which is called Sunday, all who live in the cities or in the countryside gather together in one place. And the memoirs of the apostles or the writings of the prophets are read as long as there is time. Then, when the reader has finished, the president [presiding minister], in a discourse, admonishes and invites the people to practice these examples of virtue. Then we all stand up together and offer prayers. And, as we mentioned before, when we have finished the prayer, bread is presented, and wine with water; the president likewise offers up prayers and thanksgivings according to his ability, and the people assent by saying, Amen. The elements which have been "eucharistized" are distributed and received by each one; and they are sent to the absent by the deacons. Those who are prosperous, if they wish, contribute what each one deems appropriate; and the collection is deposited with the president; and he takes care of the orphans and widows, and those who are needy because of sickness or other cause, and the captives, and the strangers who sojourn amongst us — in brief, he is the curate of all who are in need. Sunday, indeed, is the day on which we all hold our common assembly, inasmuch as it is the first day on which

God, transforming the darkness and matter, created the universe; and on the same day our Saviour Jesus Christ rose from the dead.

This vivid portrait shows us the Christian community at its Sunday worship. At the same time it reveals the church people's life in ministry and mission. The very shape and content of their celebration of Scriptures and the meal is integral to the form and dynamism of their serving others. Here worship is clearly the way of remembering and receiving the self-giving of God, which propels them to be signs of living prayer and service to others.

Can there be any doubt, in light of this remarkable still photograph, of the inner relationship between the community gathered to celebrate eucharist and the community's life of caretaking and ministry? The people seem caught up into the simple rhythm of gathering and greeting, reading and listening to Scripture, preaching and responding to the sermon, praying for the world, presenting the bread baked in their homes and brought to this place along with the wine, offering praise and thanksgiving together, breaking the bread and distributing the sacramental signs, sharing these and all their gifts with those in need, and then scattering into their domestic and public lives in the sure conviction that God created all things, who in Jesus Christ, dying and rising, has redeemed the world. How Christians pray and how they are to be related — to one another, to all in suffering and need, and to the whole created order — these are intrinsic to what is remembered and celebrated.

What brought these people together for common worship about the font, the book — shall we say, the "living memories" — and the table was not simply the desire to satisfy personal needs. Neither was it a matter of wanting religious consolation and fellowship with God. These matters could, after all, be accomplished by private devotion and individual prayer. The real driving force, the urgency of gathering together in this way, arose out of the very nature of the Christian faith itself. Sunday gathering for the Word and the prayers and the Lord's Supper was an identity-conferring activity. It literally was a manifestation of who they were and who they were yet to become.

The grace of Christ which had overwhelmed Jesus' followers in the resurrection appearances, such as that reported in Luke 24 on the road to Emmaus and throughout Luke-Acts, continued to be encountered most powerfully in their coming together as a corporate body. Paul's metaphor of the body of Christ with many members suddenly takes on alarming concreteness. For the Sunday eucharist was literally a re-membering: that is, a putting together of the body of believers who were to be Christ for the world. The Church was constituted by its eucharistic gatherings in a way that gave persons memory, hope, compassion, and strength for the journey. Each Lord's Day, Christians are invited to experience anew the encounter with Jesus. Each day and every day is thus to be configured in what we do together as a corporate body in worship. As Dwight Vogel has said in *Food For Pilgrims*, "...we need to start with an insistence that the celebration of the sacraments is not tangential to the life of the Church, but at its very center."

The new covenant about which Jesus spoke, and which the Church claimed he enacted and shares in the meal in the context of his suffering and death, is not given to isolated individuals but to members of the body. Through the New Testament this conception of the Church as one body of many members flashes forth in great power. We cannot but be impressed with how Paul, reflecting upon the nature of authentic worship in light of the misunderstandings rampant at Corinth, returns again and again to this governing image. It was in the corporate worship patterned along the synagogue liturgy of the Word and this fourfold pattern that the redemptive power and spiritual journey of life with God in Christ was clearly manifest — so much so that the Eastern churches to this day speak of worship as an *epiphany*, a manifestation of all that Christ was and is. No wonder the Roman imperial authorities were upset and sought to obliterate Christianity by preventing Christians from meeting together for worship — above all, for these strange "rites" with bread and wine.

The New Testament and the first documents of the early Church manifest the meaning and the impact of this simple meal on the life and order of the young and growing churches. As Dom Gregory Dix observed in *The Shape of the Liturgy*, the eucharist "had trained and sanctified apostles and martyrs and scores of thousands of unknown saints for more than a century before the New Testament was collected and canonised as authoritative 'scripture,' beside and above the old jewish [sic] scriptures" (p. 3).

This common essential action was what one did after confession and training and initiation by water and the Spirit into the Church. Strikingly, of the four actions, three are essentially nonverbal: the taking (offering of gifts), the breaking of the bread, and the sharing of the "eucharistized" (blessed) gifts of bread and wine. The second of the four is a special kind of action of the whole community: the great prayer of thanksgiving over the bread and the cup. This form of prayer emerged from already practiced and well-known Hebrew prayer forms, most notably prayers of blessing, praise, thanksgiving, and supplication. Remember how the prayers in synagogue characteristically open: "Blessed be thou, O Lord, King of the universe, who bringest forth food from the earth." "Blessed be thou, who exaltest them that are lowly." "Blessed be thou, . . . who clothest the naked." These prayers present a sustained activity of acknowledging God in all particular occasions. By praising God or blessing the name of God, the things named or recounted were thus sanctified. So every occasion might be regarded as a manifestation of God's mercy, justice, or loving-kindness. The continual glorification of the name of God in every circumstance is itself a pattern of acknowledging all God's works of creating and redeeming. The way in which things were made holy was not so much to ask God to "bless" them as to offer them to God and bless God's name for them.

This carries over into the earliest forms of the eucharistic prayer itself. The essential element in these prayers was a recalling of the mighty works of God in creation and history. Yet this is no mere memory of a fixed past; rather, the prayers remember and proclaim what God is now doing. What is remembered and recited in thanksgiving and praise and supplication is part of the present encounter of the actuality of God's presence. In this sense, the eucharistic prayers of the early Church were the most profound utterance of theology and spirituality: a living remembrance that "consecrated" and sanctified the ordinary gifts of bread and wine and enabled the community by faith to discern the power and presence of God in Christ. What Jesus said and did in his earthly ministry, he *now* says and does.

Rediscovering the Holy Meal

How, then, may we rediscover in our time and place the richness for theology and the spiritual life of the sacrament of the Lord's Supper? Precisely by seeing that the actions at the table are themselves focal points for the whole range of our experience. Our sense of gratitude and hope, our joys and sufferings, our living and our dying are in this meal and in these actions given back to us. But we must be prepared to enter fully into the life Jesus calls us to live if we are to celebrate the eucharistic meal faithfully. Entering his pattern of life: teaching, healing, feeding, comforting, suffering for others, speaking the truth in love — all these and more are what we must begin to live in our daily lives if we are to grasp what is given in the sacrament of the table.

At the same time, the fourfold action itself provides us with the key to the pattern of our lives lived in company with Jesus. We offer ourselves as a "living sacrifice of praise and thanksgiving." The offering is ours because it is first given to us. Our lives do not take on meaning and deep joy until they are given for others. So we offer ourselves, as the old prayerbook language has it, "our souls and bodies, to be a reasonable and holy sacrifice." This is because we first acknowledge our very existence as a gift from God. Indeed, in the Christian life we say that we can only love God and give ourselves to God because "Christ first loved us." Giving ourselves over to the mercy and to the compassion of the One who created all things and called them good is to discover our own best being. This discovery is so powerful that it is called "conversion." So we take all that we are — whoever and in whatsoever condition we find ourselves — and offer them to God. Just so, God has given us gifts of bread and wine from the goodness of creation to offer. This is the hidden meaning of the often-sung offering phrase: "We give Thee but thine own, whate'er the gift may be: all that we have is Thine alone, a trust, O Lord, from Thee."

For those who know the story of Jesus, this self-giving is based on more than the creative goodness of God, as though that were not reason enough. It is rooted and grounded in the incomprehensible fact of God's own self-giving in the life, passion, and death of Jesus Christ. Thus we can present ourselves before God, along with the created elements of bread and wine, for transformation because God has expressed solidarity with us and all humankind in Christ. This is a double mystery: the first, that the very stuff of creation is sanctified and manifest as holy by acknowledging it before the Creator; the second, that human beings — so far alienated from ourselves and our own true destiny and being — may be made holy and alive and well by offering in the strong name of Jesus Christ. The God who creates is the God who saves. Take, offer — this is the way to life, and the way to gratitude and thanksgiving and love of God.

The act of the great thanksgiving is what our lives are meant to be. As some of the early theologians of the Church have said, the whole life of a Christian should be a continuous prayer to God. This is the pattern Jesus confers. All our doings, all our becomings, are found in God. Christian spirituality is, in this light, a continuing dialogue with God and a continuing discovery of whom we are meant to be for one another. So we may follow in our own lives the structure of the ancient eucharistic prayers: acknowledge God in praise for who God is, a mystery of being yet a furnace of compassion, our creator hidden in glory yet revealed in the whole created order, if we have eyes to see and ears to hear. Then we acknowledge God's holiness, "Holy, Holy, Holy, Lord God of power and might. Heaven and earth are full of your glory."

And, as the prayer of thanksgiving develops, so do our lives. We remember all the mighty works of God in creation, covenant, and redemptive history. But we also remember our alienation, our turning aside, our own history in God's presence and absence. Our lives come to light and to identity the more we enter into this story of God prayed by the community. In everyday life we are to be the places of living memory — telling the truth and reminding ourselves and the world of God's intention for us. It is in the context of our lives that we discern, if at all, what it means to remember that Christ, on the night in which he was betrayed, took bread and took the cup. In the midst of our desolation and complicity and bitter denial and death-dealing and hope for a society of justice and peace, we may begin to understand what we remember when we remember him. His teachings for our light, his body and blood our sin, strangely become our food and drink for life and eternal hope.

To live is to call upon God the Holy Spirit, breathed upon the disciples and upon the whole community and upon all who, in him, pray to God with their lives, "Lord, send forth your Spirit, and renew the face of the earth." To the great "Amen" our lives lean, seeking a final blessing and a restoration to final well-being. This is the way of eucharistic praying. This is the way of eucharistic living.

But our lives, too, must be broken open. Just as the bread is broken in order to be shared, so we must be prepared to be given for others. The image of the bread, itself composed of wheat and kneaded by hands over a process of growth and maturing — this it is we are to be come for God's world. We are, by virtue of our deepest calling, to be bread for others. Our God is truly prodigal, a spendthrift God who sets a feast before us, even in our ordinariness, to be a feast for others. So we must be speaking and touching and feeding and reconciling in God's name; we are to be sowers of seed and bakers of bread, wonderfully given to a world of need.

But — and this is the most terrifying and beautiful matter — through this form of life we receive back our own lives. It is our own mystery which Christ has given back to us in the humble signs of bread and wine, in the whole gathered community in word and gesture and meal. Grace is given in the eucharist, but this is the grace we also encounter in offering, blessing, breaking open, and sharing our lives to all this needy world. This is our lost identity; this is the secret hidden from the eyes of the detached and self-possessed world.

Six

Remembering The World to God

*Remember, Lord, Christians at sea, on the road, abroad, our fathers and broth-
ers [and sisters] in chains and prisons, in captivity and exile, in mines and
tortures and bitter slavery; for a peaceful return home for each of them.*

*Remember, Lord, those in old age and infirmity, those who are sick, ill, or
troubled by unclean spirits, for their speedy healing and salvation by you, their
God....*

*Remember, Lord, all . . . for good; on all have mercy. Master, reconcile us all,
bring peace to the multitudes of your peoples, disperse the scandals, abolish
wars, and the divisions of the churches, speedily put down the uprisings of the
heresies, . . . grant us your peace and your love, God our saviour, the hope of
all the ends of the earth.*

These words are strong and fresh. They might well be prayed by
modern communities of faith under suffering and persecution in parts
of our world. Yet they come from the prayers of the early Church; to
be precise, from the liturgy of St. James, the text of which dates from
about 400. It was doubtless prayed in the intercessions of some early
churches well back into the fourth century.

We begin by joining with these ancient prayers of petition because they express a central feature of Christian spirituality. To pray
with the Church is to remember the world before God, to be in dialogue with God about the suffering and yearnings of all God's
creatures. To pray such petitions and to intend them faithfully is to
embody a way of life in solidarity with all for whom Christ bids us
pray. In this way our spirituality is nourished in the truth of holding

69

the world steadily before God. To pray as members of Christ's body — those baptized into his death and resurrection — is to undertake a way of becoming present to the world's wildfire and ambiguity as well as its grandeur and mystery. To pray for the world in communion with all creatures is to journey into the very heart of God's presence to the world. To intercede for the world is to be with Jesus Christ present in the midst of his people. To remember the world before God is to stand in solidarity with all the wide earth: its sinfulness and suffering and its terrible beauty.

Praying for Others

Spirituality in this key does not depend upon having the right "theory" about the relation between prayer and life in service to neighbor. Rather, it requires a vision of their profound unity in God. For all our life with God and unto God is a holy surrender of ourselves in union with Christ's self-offering in obedience and love to God, whom he calls "Abba," Father. Everything we have yet to discover about embodying a way of life, about our hope, our reason for being, and our responsibility, is grounded in praying with Christ. This is why Henri Nouwen and others have spoken of our common ministry as becoming "living reminders of Jesus Christ" to the world.

Have you ever wondered why we are alternately moved and bored by "pastoral prayers"? Sometimes, in free church Protestantism as well as in more liturgical churches, the extended prayer of the pastor or of a layperson on all our behalf touches deeply into our experience and helps us express our petitions to God. "O God, we remember before you this day our brother Jim and our sister Mary, and all others who struggle with cancer, that they may be strengthened and surrounded by your healing love and mercy for the days ahead." And we say in our hearts, "Amen." When the prayers touch us, we are reminded of our ministries and we are able to unburden ourselves.

Yet we are often prevented from prayer because the leader of prayer is lost in some abstract scheme of adoration, confession, thanksgiving, petition, and blessing or is simply offering the personal ramblings of his or her unconsidered, thoughtless consciousness. These are the times of impatience, and the times when intercession as remembering the world unto God is prevented. Public prayer does indeed give us patterns of our own interior prayers for others. This is why the pastoral prayer traditions in many of our churches need a new mutuality between people and leaders. Each gathering of Christians focuses upon our prayers for others and for the world, whether in the daily prayer offices, the informal house prayers, the litany at baptisms and confirmations, or the intercessions between the Word and eucharistic meal each Lord's Day. In this sense all gatherings for worship must enable us to remember the world before God. Thereby the meaning of baptism is manifest and the significance of the holy meal is deepened. The link between praising God, the thankful remembering of what God has done, and supplicating God on behalf of the world is essential. As long as synagogues and churches have an unclear sense or a diminished practice of these inner connections, our spirituality is impoverished.

Remembering the world before God is, as we have seen, a profound feature of biblical worship and life. The psalmist is bold in lamenting the suffering, the injustice, and the brokenness of human life. There is language of human suffering expressed here, which we avoid at our peril: pain, grief, anger, dismay, desolation — these too are addressed to God. "I am poured out like water . . .; my strength is dried up like a potsherd" (Ps. 22:14-15). "My enemies trample upon me all day long" (56:2). And all these human experiences, personal and social, are boldly spoken to God in supplication and lament: God, listen to our prayer! "Be not far from me" (22:11). "O God, . . . remember thy congregation" (74:1-2). This is the reality of remembering with the psalmist and, indeed, with the whole biblical tradition. So, along with the remembrance of God's mighty acts, and the happy times of peace and prosperity, there is at the heart of faith this confrontation with the pain, the anxiety, and the precariousness of life–both of our own and of those around us. To remember life before God with the psalms is, as Walter Brueggemann has reminded us in *Praying the Psalms,* always a movement "between *the pit* and *the wing,* between the shattering of disorientation and the gift of life" (p. 47).

Prayer As Solidarity

Our lives are incomplete until we learn solidarity with others who suffer, who are pressed down, who are desolate, but who also rejoice. Only in this way can we cease being alienated from our own experience of these things. Christian spirituality begins a deeper perception of the "tragic sense of life," to use Miguel deUnamuno's phrase, but always as part of the journey toward God. There can be no true prayer without such radical identification; no true serving of others without praying for them; no true praying for them without sharing, literally sharing, their sorrows, griefs, burdens, and joys.

For this reason we should take heart that various worship and liturgical reforms among several church traditions have restored the prayers of the people, or the general intercessions, to a central role on Sunday. The discovery that the laity can and must pray for others in our gathered worship is crucial to growth in spiritual discernment. While the clergy have their enabling role and indeed may characteristically preside over the intercessions, only by the whole body of believers "owning" these prayers can depth of connection between worship and ministry, between liturgy and life, be renewed. We are not at the whim of the spiritual strength of priests and pastors; we are here invited to lift our world to the creator and redeemer of all things precisely because Christ is in our midst praying with us and for us. Or, as Paul says, "the Spirit . . . intercedes for us with sighs too deep for words." It is true we do not know how to pray as we ought, but we do come together to begin again and again. Yet we are not to come empty-handed before God. We come with our human experiences of the suffering and rejoicing of our world. In some mysterious sense, we can not hold that, or even know what it is we suffer with the world, until we remember these things before God.

The words from James Weldon Johnson's hymn express the address of a particular people's history to God in the form also of supplication: "God of our weary years, God of our silent tears, / Thou who hast brought us thus far on the way, / Thou who hast by Thy might, led us into the light, / Keep us forever in the path, we pray."

Such a remembering of the specific pain of the history of black people in America is also a redemptive prayer. It is a sign of intercession born of a story that white Christians should also remember with repentance. The recognition of Christ in the power of the Spirit in baptism and in eucharist carries over to our common prayer. To recognize him in worship is to confess Christ also in the world, in the hurt and pain of the neighbor. We may resist such a connection. Most of us do not recognize the relation between prayer and ministry until we have encountered this outside the rooms of worship. It is nonetheless real and permanent.

As I have tried to express in *The Soul in Paraphrase (p.* 98), our intercessions as praying for the world should thus be marked with the awareness of God's presence in the world:

> As Christ had compassion, so must we; as he encountered the brokenness of his children, so must we; as he loved, even in the face of death, so must we.... The intercessions are the practice and the exercise of *being turned* so that we look in the direction that God's love is looking . . . away from self, and away from the Church's in-house preoccupations.

Our impoverished experience of common prayer for the world is directly traceable to our inability to know and to minister to others in his name. Common prayer fails because of our insulation from others' brokenness and our numerous fears and self-doubts. At the same time, all our social ministry in the world will never sustain Christ's presence unless we have times and places of *ritual focus* upon what Christ is now doing. Intercessory prayer and the common prayer for others is, like the whole range of Christian liturgy, our "school for ministry." And our ministries must be the stuff of prayer.

A traditional problem in spirituality is the so-called tension between action and contemplation, between prayer and doing ministry. But such distinctions are misleading. Not all prayer is contemplative or passive. And surely not all ministry is active. We all know times of being ministered unto in our very act of serving others. It is a matter of our discovering the various rhythms of activity and passivity, of attending and struggling and receiving, *within* our praying and ministering.

One day several months ago, as I was visiting a former student who is now a pastor in Florida, Gary told me, "Today we are going to see Myrtie." We drove to the place where she lived, a one-story, institutional-looking brick building that was obviously a home for the elderly.

We passed through the doors into a world of wheelchairs and nursing stations and the sounds and smells of the places where so many of our old people now stay. Walking down the hall, we passed the silent, palsied ones, and the talkative ones with holiday ornaments on their house dresses, and the many antiseptic rooms with nothing but the omnipresent television set to lend them life.

Then we came to Myrtie's room. She was sitting up in bed, the third bed, closest to the window. When we approached she looked up and said, "Oh, boy." My friend greeted her and introduced me, to which she responded quietly, "Oh, boy." "We've brought you some surprises from your friends in the church." "Oh, boy." The reply sparkled. The presents were each laboriously unwrapped by her one usable hand and each received a soft or surprised "Oh, boy."

The news of the church was shared with her — births and deaths and bean suppers and worship — and then Gary opened the little case with the small piece of bread and the small cup, into which some wine was poured. "The body of Christ; the cup of salvation." "Oh, boy," she responded, so prayerfully it brought us near tears. Then came some further conversation, a brief expression of pain with her two syllables, the exchange of kisses to the cheek, and our final goodbyes. "We'll see you again, Myrtie." "Oh, boy," was her farewell to us. After we left, and just as we were getting into the car outside a window of the building, I caught sight of her through the curtains, looking at us from her place, her good hand waving ever so slightly and her mouth forming "O" and "B."

Then it was I learned that she had suffered a stroke allowing her only two sounds. But oh, what a language: such welcoming, such pain, such directness, such memory, and such a sign to us talkative ones!

This is what we mean when we talk about prayer both in words and beyond words. This is what we mean when we say that ministry in action is often stopped in astonishment by the contemplative beholding of God in the little ones and the "least of these." This is why we can never divide prayer and ministry into separate parts of our lives, or make action for some and contemplation for others.

Recall again that in Scripture, especially in the Law and the Prophets, to obey God's commands is a form of remembering who God is. To recite the marvels of God in the liturgy is necessary. But to care for the orphan and the widow and to give hospitality to the sojourner and the stranger are concrete ways of remembering God. Awareness of God and living communion with God are dependent upon cultic remembering *and* doing the works of justice and mercy. To do one without the other is to misunderstand the nature of God's creatures. Jesus certainly stands in this tradition when he speaks, in Matthew 25, of those who say "Lord, Lord" but who do not remember God by doing the works of mercy. As Dwight Vogel says, "We eat and drink the labor of others. To the extent that their labor is the result of oppression or injustice, we participate in their suffering." (*Food For Pilgrims*) Those who are able to recognize God at the end time, even though surprised, will be those who have visited the sick and imprisoned and who have fed the hungry, clothed the naked, and given the cup of water to the "least of these," Christ's brothers and sisters.

Prayer as ministry, ministry as prayer: this is more than a catchy slogan, it is what we must always and everywhere explore if we are to be faithful witnesses to our calling as a people of God who remember. We are to signify Christ to the world, even as he is given to us continually in our praying to him, in our receiving him in Word and sacrament and mission. At the heart of all Christian prayer is this living with the one mystery, which is God's life embracing us and all creation back to God. We are to serve in the name of the incarnate one revealed and revealing God's very utterance and life made flesh — a mystery still veiled from our eyes but open to our ears and our hearts.

All this is far more radical than we may first think. Such remembering of the world to God is a place of self-discovery. For, while spirituality is concerned with grace and wholeness and the inner discipline of the Spirit, we must remind ourselves that the inner life can never be, for the Christian, a private space of personal experience and consolation cultivated at the expense of our public ministries. Whatever is "inner" and "whole" is reflected in our relatedness to the actual shape of ministry wherever and whenever it becomes real.

Whatever is "inner" and "whole" is part of who we are and what we are becoming, in our daily relationships, in our family life and in our public witness and service of the gospel.

Embodied Life In The Spirit

A Christian spirituality that remains unembodied and focused only within the interior life and "religious" experience of the individual believer is both unbiblical and a dangerous deception. The spirituality we seek does have much to do with our fundamental orientation, and with the center on all our doing, feeling, and knowing. In short, it is a matter of the heart. Learning to pray more deeply and to serve God more freely and authentically is a call to the transformation of the heart, as Calvin and Wesley and Edwards and Kierkegaard and Luther and Pascal and Benedict and Augustine and Perpetua and Felicity and Polycarp and Ignatius and Paul and the apostles all knew: so we witness, so we must claim. Authentic Christian spirituality is communal, and its discipline is found in remembering the world to God. But its source is in God's remembering us. This is why any ministry without the means of grace in the gathered enactment of the story and the Church's memory is impoverished and, finally, impossible.

> For this reason I bow my knees before the Father, from whom every family in heaven and on earth takes its name. I pray that according to the riches of his glory he may grant that you may be strengthened in your inner being with power through his Spirit, and that Christ may dwell in your hearts through faith, as you are being rooted and grounded in love. I pray that you may have the power to comprehend, with all the saints, what is the breadth and length and height and depth, and to know the love of Christ that surpasses knowledge, so that you may be filled with all the fullness of God. (Eph. 3:14-19)

Few passages in Scripture rival in comprehensiveness or luminosity this ardent prayer for the life and ministry of the Church. It is a living image of the shape and character of Christian life to which the whole people of God is called. This sheds light upon that household's various ministries, as the letter to the church at Ephesus makes clear. Whatever variety of gifts for ministry have been be stowed, they are knit together and given their fundamental *telos* by the stature of the fullness of Christ, into whom "we are to grow up in every way" (Eph. 4:15). Learning Christ in his fullness is not something the Christian community could choose to do; rather, it is the indelible character of the hope to which we have been called. Not to be thus formed is to miss the reality of the Christian vocation, bestowed by baptism into Christ.

Here we must learn to live a strange paradox. Only in the conscious intention to pray together and for others can we find the environment that makes it possible to receive God in everyday life. Yet only by attending to the hidden signs of God in the suffering and the ordinary round of human relationships do we discover the conditions for praying to a living God. As Jacques Ellul observed, in *Prayer and Modern Man,* "It is prayer which creates the silence needed for prayer" (p. 68). To remember the world to God requires our being silenced before the mystery of God's presence in the lowly and the everyday. To be silenced is to listen for what God may have to say to our petitions and our supplications.

Seeking God so easily takes the form of disembodied wishful thinking, or a self-indulgent set of experiential consolations. Such an attempt to live the religious life substitutes daydreaming for being awake to God; it substitutes sentimentality and reverie for remembering and real encounter. If there are any fruits of the Spirit that come from remembering the world to God, these can never be private consolations. For only in our solidarity with those for whom and with whom we pray can we learn the deeper affections and virtues of joy and thanksgiving and fear and repentance and hope. These are the indelibly human qualities of life, which come only by the journey of interceding for the world.

All this is, of course, but another manifestation of Christ's ongoing intercession for the world. For us he was baptized, suffered, put to death; for us he rose from the dead, ascended, and now reigns and intercedes from on high.

None of us should be surprised that Christian prayer and Christian life are whole cloth, despite our continuing struggle to make them fit! Unless prayer responds to the world of ambiguity, it cannot fully fathom the world of glory. Unless we are grounded in the love of God in Christ who remembers us despite our forgetfulness, and despite all the world can do to kill body and spirit, we are not prepared to live fully. To receive the wholeness God seeks to give requires our pleading the world to God. God never wishes to reduce our humanity to automatic responses, much less to coerced submission. But God remembers "that we are but dust" and gives us a way of transformation, sanctification, and glorification.

We are to pray and we are to become prayerful in all that we do. This is a task and a gift. This is our liturgy. For God desires us to call the world to love, the divine love; in this mysterious sense God has made covenant to need us. And we, poor creatures of brokenness and alienation from the sources of our own love and compassion, can still pray, with Gerard Manley Hopkins, "Because the Holy Ghost over the bent World broods with warm breast and with ah! bright wings."

Seven

The Shape of Things to Come

"Behold, I make all things new."
REVELATION 21:5

Who among us has not yearned for a community of human beings in which love of neighbor, justice, and peace were no longer a dream but a reality? At one time or another we all have an intense longing for the ideal society, for a beloved community. From time to time a prophetic voice arises in our midst to put in words the unexpressed fire we feel: "I have a dream!"

In times of great stress and social uncertainty such as our own, it does not take much to trigger the desire for a world made just and well. Individualism fails us, and the culture of self-preoccupation will, soon or late, leave us empty. "Lately I have felt so empty; nothing I do, or that anyone around me does, stays in place. I feel deserted and afraid." This from the lips of a bright, sensitive seminary student. Have we not all known something of this self preoccupation, which is seemingly forced upon us because so few persons or institutions appear to support our deepest desires and aspirations? Despair sometimes grows from too much awareness.

For the morally sensitive pilgrims of our age, the world of increasing awareness of the pain and suffering of others seems to lead away from trust. Either we are driven to survivalist enclosure, literally or psychologically, or we are brought to the pitch of yearning for what *ought* to be in human existence. When wars and rumors of wars bombard our every waking moment and haunt our sleep, we slide toward despair. Or, just perhaps, this desert time may be the turning point. When we taste the corn husks of the "far country," the time of awareness of our home and what we were meant to be may dawn.

If we begin to speak of a time when the nations shall not "learn war any more," we are already searching for something beyond the literal appearance of things. Already we speak in images and symbols. The connection with the hidden languages of our common human experience of suffering and mystery may be remade, and a new attentiveness to the prophet's words is possible: "and his name will be called Wonderful Counselor, Mighty God . . . the Prince of Peace." We may rediscover what has been in our common worship all along, with only the beholder wanting. What is this deep drive in us toward a reality only expressible through common belonging to story, image, song, and symbol? Therein lies a secret, the secret source of Christian spirituality.

Envisioning The Gathered Community

Central to Christian faith and life is the symbol of the gathered community. The assembly of persons, gathered in the name of God about the font, the book, and the table, symbolizes another society beyond our human dreams. It points toward and manifests another community beyond the tired politics of the world and even beyond the dreams of the Church. Here we confront a symbol for the relation of all humankind in restored relation to one another and to the whole of the created order. This has always been the very stuff of prophetic imagination. "The descendants of those who oppressed you shall come bending low to you; . . . they shall call you the City of the Lord, the Zion of the Holy One of Israel" (Isa. 60:14). John the Seer writes, "Then I saw a new heaven and a new earth.... And I saw the holy city, the new Jerusalem, coming down out of heaven from God" (Rev. 21:1-2). Is there something, after all, to these dreams and visions? Were not these given to the funded memories of God's people, embedded and often obscured in our liturgies?

We know all too well that the Church does not exemplify such a vision in its life, nor does it often allow the expression of such universal human hope in its preaching and ministries. Yet our hope is nothing less than that for which no community, including particular church traditions, has ever yet realized fully in time and space. Nevertheless, the symbol is there and it is real beyond our imagination's reach. The new city, the New Jerusalem in which "all is just and all is right," is sought after again and again in Jewish and Christian prophetic vision. In the liturgies of the gathered people of God, such a story of our future is narrated and kept alive. Yet, if we know how to enter into the mystery and the pain of the narrative, we will find the hope as well. Redemptive memory bestows an actual change in disposition and rescues us from bondage to the fixity of the past history of our own making.

Authentic worship trains us for the reign of God yet to come in a society of justice and peace. The symbol is given in the midst of suffering and injustice. The vision of the divine rule preached by Jesus is the Kingdom already changing us and yet to come. The mystery hidden from the plain view is found in the worship life of those who choose to remember God with the prophets, apostles, martyrs, and the whole company of those whom God has named. Where there is no deep memory, no participation in the history of suffering and hope, but only sentiment and the recall of fixed experience, there can be no true in vocation, thanksgiving, supplication, and sustained hope.

In the traditions of Israel and in the Church, hope for the rule of God and the advent of justice and peace became focused and expressed in the meal — a human community gathered to invoke, to speak, to break the bread, and to share life with God. In Christianity, Jesus continues this hope by embodying it. He reconfigures it with his own life and death. The bread broken and shared is his summation of all that God speaks through the Law and the Prophets. The cup shared is his life's blood of longing and obedience and compassion poured out upon the whole world. So he takes, blesses, breaks, and shares.

In celebrating this meal with his companions, Jesus *enacts* the hope for glory and the reconciliation of human beings to one another and to God. The eucharistic words and actions of the gathered faithful are a faithful continuation of Jesus' own self-giving now. What he said and did then, he now says and does in the midst of us. Our deepest experiences and convictions carry us out toward what the meal itself points us toward — all gathered about God's table. To "do this in remembrance" is therefore to participate in much more powerful forms of emotion and intention and imagination than our conventional Sunday-School faith can say.

Living Between The Times

The problem, however, is that we have not grasped the interrelationship between remembering and becoming what God has already begun to do in our midst. The neglect of the disciplines of time in daily prayers of morning and evening, the loss of the Church year as a continuing living of the narrative of God's history with us and the story of Jesus' life, ministry, suffering, and death/resurrection, and the loss of vital sacramental faith and biblical preaching — all these have conspired to diminish our sense of the way in which the Christian life remembers and becomes something more than it already is.

The rebirth of interest in spirituality must also be a rediscovery of eschatology, not merely as the doctrine of the end times but precisely as a way of living and worshiping. To understand that what in us as we now are must die begins with baptism. What in our lives of alienation, bitterness, self-preoccupation, intolerance, vengeance seeking, and the subtle weave of lies and broken promises must be put to death? What in our public responsibilities must be exorcised and changed? What in our wasteful ways must be put away, and what new garments of simplicity, truthfulness, and openness to God must be put on? These questions have not been asked strenuously enough in our baptismal practices; and the disciplines of time, personal integrity, contemplative space, and wonder are rarely part of what the Church expects of its experience of conversion! As we saw in Chapter Five, indiscriminate baptism and lackluster faith formation deny the power of Christ's dying and rising.

What must be appreciated and reintroduced into our common life is the conception of living between the times. The means of grace — prayer, searching Scripture, the sacraments, fasting, acts of love and mercy — are themselves eschatological. We remember the God who is yet to come. What is given in baptism, growth into the mystery of love, and the repentant heart, is our capacity for God's future. This is always a social holiness. It involves the rediscovery of solidarity in the world's corporate sinfulness and release for guilt and sin to serve cheerfully. The baptismal waters are death-dealing and life-giving: the death of our old ways, the coming-to-birth of the new.

When Jesus, into whose life and suffering and death/resurrection we are baptized, stands now in our midst to break the bread and pour out the cup, this is a promise and portent of the messianic blessings yet to come. Here lives are patterned on the old baptismal confession, the Apostolic Creed. As we share in his death, so we shall yet be made alive. As he ascended, so are we invited to journey toward God. But we are not alone. The whole suffering, yearning world is also summoned in our journey. This is the only true basis for evangelical witness: that we are to be living reminders of God's future for all people, for the whole cosmos, which, as Paul says, groans in travail for the liberation from bondage to sin and death. In what sense have we begun this journey if our common life is so far removed from what is given in the means of grace?

In a world of death-dealing and deceit, what does it mean to acclaim, "Dying, you destroyed our death / Rising you restored our life / Lord Jesus, come in glory!"? What does it mean to cry on behalf of the whole world, *"Maranatha!"*? To this we now turn.

"I can't accept a piety that tells us everything is all right, and that Jesus has made everything O.K. if we only have enough faith, when the world and the Church is torn apart and dishonest." She had finally reached a point in her own life when she could, as she put it, "no longer afford to be dishonest about the things I care for most deeply." So, in her assessment, she shared with us her sense of dissatisfaction with the conventional church life she had experienced and tolerated so long. This person, who had put so many years of faithful, loving service into "church work" and who had seen several pastors come and go with their own versions of the gospel, now wanted to level with us. What does the spiritual life mean when so much of the Church's practice and theology is a "piety that tells us everything is all right"?

First, not everything is all right, especially for people of faith and hope. In *The Longing for Home*, Frederick Buechner issues a warning: "Woe to all of us if we stay only in the bright uplands of the Gospels and avoid like death, avoid like life, the dark ravines, the cave under the hill." (p. 130). The Scriptures show this; the psalmist laments it. The very way of life we are called to live is likely to see more of the darkness than a way of life that has no profession of "the Light of the world." If we make compromises with how things are, or cultivate a detached cynicism, the world need not yield any being "surprised by grace."

But we must go on to observe that the passion of faith raises precisely that woman's question. We must come to terms with the realities in our lives and in our institutional arrangements because another way of life is offered. In that group we discussed the idea that those who profess Jesus to have come in the flesh have already gotten a taste for the Kingdom — for the rule and reign of God's Shalom. Just because of this "foretaste of glory divine" we must become discontent with the pain and the injustice so evident in our world.

Then something dawned upon her and all in the room with her. This is exactly how it is with God; that is how it was and is with Jesus! Our foretaste of what God intends for the whole creation is also a recognition that the Kingdom has *not* come in fullness. Christ has come in the flesh — this we confess; but he has not returned in glory. Such a return is not a matter of some last-day fireworks. Rather, he seeks to be present in fullness in every time and place where his body gathers. The very cry *Maranatha!* — *"Come,* Lord!" — shows that Jesus' death and resurrection points toward that which is not yet. So baptism and eucharist point toward that which we must live toward. The Lord's Supper, and any spiritual life grounded therein, proclaims "the Lord's death until he comes" (I Cor. 11:26). So every real encounter with Christ and every real act of love in the world is anticipatory. To put it squarely: Jesus Christ is already present in our prayer and our service, making God known through the Holy Spirit in which we dwell. Yet at the same time he is absent: absent in the way we all know in our suffering. In this way all Christian praying, all baptisms, all celebrations of Word and the Lord's Supper tell us about the future. The discontent is not a failure of faith but a sign of it! Even more, authentic faith already anticipates God's future by living in the tension of relating to God and neighbor in a world not yet ready. We live in a world still fully bent on its own deathly kingdoms.

So, too, the waters of baptism give life while creating turbulence for us and for our world. The waters of baptism may yet unloose the foundations of all forms of power that are untruth. The meal of eucharist is bread and wine for the future as well as for the daily journey. In some strange and not fully comprehensible way, we must learn to live in a future becoming present. But that requires living memory, suffering, and a sense of mystery. We are sustained by God, but always by manna that is *daily.* This is what Jesus meant in teaching us to pray, "Give us this day our daily bread." The bread for our nourishment is God's Word, and it is also the bread which anticipates Christ's full presence. So we also pray, "Hasten the day when all shall gather about your table in the Kingdom." Then we suddenly see how our acts of love and works of mercy are given new orientation and humanity. God is present in, with, and through them. To live toward God's vision for the future demands our humanity at full stretch; nevertheless, "It is no longer I who live, but it is Christ who lives in me" (Gal. 2:20).

Remember, then, what Augustine said in his famous prayer in the *Confessions:* "Thou hast made us for thyself and restless is our heart until it comes to rest in thee." This discontent, even the moral pain we undergo in the gap between what faith promises and how the world actually is — this restlessness is itself a sign of God's justice and mercy. In the midst of a forgetful, unheeding, yet bleeding and dying world, we have this gifted restlessness. We have this vocation to be a covenant people and to be living reminders in our worship and our call to social holiness.

Yet in the travail of honest spirituality for our lives today, we can never forget that he has promised us peace in the midst of all such striving. In the midst of frightened, anxious men and women he comes, as of old, saying, "Fear not; peace I give you." Such peace is more real than the self-destructive and cynical ways in which we all "make our peace with how things are."

This is why Christian spirituality must be once again in our time rooted and grounded in the liturgy, Christ's liturgy in and through us. This is why with boldness we may speak to God and cry, "Remember your servants, Lord; remember your people, O Lord. Do not desert us. Make haste to hear us, make speed to save us." To this the love of God says, "How can I forget you? How can I give you up?" For God will remember us and call out, "Hear, O my people, remember that I am that Lord your God who created you and gave you life and delivered you from captivity." Remember whose we are.

Feast For All Peoples

The Kingdom of God is portrayed often in Scripture as a feast. The prophets envisioned this. So Isaiah: "On this mountain the LORD of hosts will make for all peoples a feast of rich food, a feast of well-aged wines" and "will swallow up death forever. Then the LORD GOD will wipe away the tears from all faces, and the disgrace of his people he will take away from all the earth" (Isa. 25:6, 8). In the desert one pictures redemption and well-being as an oasis; in the time of starvation and widespread hunger, a feast. For us who already are too fat with our own consumption, this is an ambiguous picture. The prophetic word to all who search for God who are already satisfied with this world's goods is that we must learn to fast and to go the desert way in order to understand what God has prepared for all people, and for us.

The same prophet calls out to us:

Is not this the fast that I choose:
to loose the bonds of injustice,
to undo the thongs of the yoke,

to let the oppressed go free,
and to break every yoke?
Is it not to share your bread with the hungry,
and bring the homeless poor into your house;
when you see the naked, to cover them,
and not to hide yourself from your own kin?

(Isa. 58:6-7)

Are we not reminded again of the sayings of Jesus in Matthew 25? It is the mark of the Christian life to ask "Lord, when did we see you, and give you drink, when did we see you and visit you in prison?" The eschatology is in our lives directed by Christ toward those occasions when God appears in the broken forms of humanity. They themselves can teach us the way toward the Kingdom. Could this be what Jesus meant in his preaching: "Blessed are the poor in spirit . . . blessed are those who mourn . . . blessed are those who hunger and thirst for righteousness"? So the rule and reign of God for which we long when our hearts and minds are uncluttered is close at hand. Is this, too, part of the mystery hid from the eyes of the world? Suppose that our whole lives are to be lived under the signs and toward the meaning of the prayer: "Thy kingdom come, thy will be done, on earth as it is in heaven"?

Yes, the Kingdom is pictured as a feast for all peoples. People "will come from east and west, from north and south, and will eat in the kingdom of God" (Luke 13:29). Yes, but "the kingdom of God is not food and drink but righteousness and peace and joy in the Holy Spirit," Paul reminds us in Romans 14:17. There is the tension. It is permanent. It is the difficult connection for all of us who live in well-appointed places with enough to eat and drink and wear. If there is to be any true "foretaste of glory divine," as the old evangelical hymn sings, it will be because our lives are made eucharist and become baptismal signs for all people. Only when our spirituality grows toward the Kingdom yet to come by being disposed to God's justice, peace, and joy in the Holy Spirit will we be fit for life with God, here and hereafter.

Beyond This Life

But something more remains, something beyond the call for us to manifest the life of the Spirit in what God has yet to bring to this earth in fullness. We are meant for this feast, just as we were meant for one another, as we are meant for life with God. But as long as we are *here* in time and space and human history, the tension between what is and what God intends will remain. "I have worked and we have struggled for peace, and we continue to work for reconciliation here," a Presbyterian elder said in my hearing to the session of a local congregation, "but we get very, very tired and hurt in the process. I think that there is more to life with God than our 'bringing in the Kingdom.' " He was pointing to an essential truth. We look for the resurrection and the life to come. We do not bring in the Kingdom by force. We ask for forgiveness; and we acknowledge that, finally, heaven is our destination.

But how shall we conceive this? How can we avoid the simple-minded piety that speaks of heaven and perpetuates hell on earth? A piety that preaches "pie in the sky" and winks at the very conditions here which drive people to the "opiate of the people"? How, indeed, except by submitting again in wonder and awe to what Jesus has ushered into our midst? His liturgy for us is our sacrament of life. His love for us is fellowship in the Spirit with the blessed community which is God. His hope for us is the consummating reconciliation of heaven and earth.

There is that which is to come, beyond whatever can be forged and experienced here and now. Heaven is not some mythological extra reward for being righteous. It is that which orients the whole narrative of human history, and saves us from our own burnt-out religiousness, whether of "interior piety" or of social justice. The Realm of God is in the process of being realized in human history, but it includes heaven and earth, which are themselves both creatures of God. Yes, even heaven. So we live as though everything depends upon how responsive the earthly is to the heavenly in our time and place. Yet we know that even "heaven and earth shall pass away." To hope for "heaven" need not be self-serving and the last bastion of religious pride. No, it is what we discover in the midst of our earthly journey. It is something for which God is preparing the whole wide earth. The liturgy, rightly understood and celebrated, lures us toward our true destiny and end: the enjoyment of God in the company of all whom God has given life.

The feasting of all created being in the love and splendor and glorious righteousness and peace of God is beyond our conceiving. It requires a transformation and a consummation. This is why holy awe and holy fear must be in the very midst of all our praise and loving deeds. Whatever we meet of God in the liturgical life of our respective churches — and we have so much more to learn — whatever we meet of God in deeds of love and mercy, there is still more. There is a place of non-separation filled with the most intense being of God. Our greatest spiritual teachers must always remind us of *beatitude,* of the blessed life, or the vision of God beyond death.

At the same time, the more our worship and work discerns the saving presence of God in Christ here, the more we become aware of what separation from God may be. God alone bestows a future. God also raises from the dead. Heaven may certainly be pictured as a place of consolation and bliss, but we know there is no "God space" that can be managed by our doctrines or by our values. Heaven is not so much walls and streets and palaces; it is the community of citizens of redemptive memory. God will remember. So our living and our dying, all our hopes and fears of beatitude and judgment, are touched when we sing of "all the saints who from their labors rest."

The powers of hell and the kingdom of death are real. Separation from God and neighbor is real enough on earth. How much more real, then, is eternal separation?

To speak of God and of heaven as the direction of human existence drawn by the grace of God is also to contemplate its opposite. Spirituality can never be full and authentically faithful if heaven is a reward based on running from hell. We are called to live toward God. This destroys the human religious project of driving people to heaven out of fear of torment and eternal damnation, however psychologically satisfying that may be to us. Rather, we worship and believe and live professing faith in God, resurrection, and eternal life. We do not profess coequal belief in condemnation and everlasting torment. Surely our lives can be filled with sobriety and solemn joy in watching and being ready, for we know not the hour of our death, nor the hour of the consummation of human history. He will come to "judge the living and the dead." But true remembering of God liberates us to orient our living and dying toward the feast.

Perhaps the most fearsome image of Satan and separation from God is found in Dante's image in the *Divine Comedy*. There Satan is found frozen eternally in the lake of ice, caught forever in the illusion of power over and against God. That the illusion of power over God and humankind is itself fearsome and destructive we have no doubt. Our own century has shown, as each day's news reveals, that the illusion of power is very destructive. Indeed, it seems to be our ultimate weapon against ourselves and the whole of the created order of God. Finally, however, the Christian community is called to worship God, not Satan. We are called to profess belief in the in-breaking kingdom, not in some apocalyptic war of good and evil. Jesus bids us take the risk of faithfulness and love of God and neighbor, which is no longer illusion but a way, a truth, and a life.

Whether we live or die, we live and die to the Lord. Remember whose you are, and who you are yet to become. Our end is in the beginning: God. Our future is in what is freely offered in the present: Christ. The journey of our life in the Spirit is found in the liturgy of Jesus Christ, in us, with us, through us. In the Spirit-giving resurrected Christ we find that the mystery, the wonder, the suffering and the glory are one. He stands as humanity's future, saying, "Behold, I make all things new."

List of Works Cited

Augustine: Confessions and Enchiridion. Translated and edited by Albert C. Outler. Volume VII in The Library of Christian Classics, edited by John Baillie, John T. McNeill, and Henry P. Van Dusen. Westminster Press, 1955.

Bell, Charles G. Cited in *A Southern Album: Recollections of Some People and Places and Times Gone By.* Edited by Irwin Glusker, narrative by Willie Morris. Oxmoor House, 1975.

Brueggemann, Walter. *Praying the Psalms.* St. Mary's Press, 1982.

Buechner, Frederick. *The Longing For Home.* San Francisco: Harper SanFrancisco. 1996.

Childs, Brevard S. *Memory and Tradition in Israel.* London: SCM Press, 1982.

Connerton, Paul. *How Societies Remember.* Cambridge: Cambridge University Press, 1989.

deUnamuno, Miguel. *The Tragic Sense of Life.* Trans. Flitch J. Crawford. New York: Dover Publications, 1921.

Dix, Gregory. *The Shape of the Liturgy.* London: Dacre Press, 1945.

Duffy, Regis. "Of Reluctant Celebrants and Reliable Symbols," *The Heythrop Journal,* Vol. 18 (1977).

Elkins, Heather Murray. *Worshiping Women:Re-Forming God's People For Praise.* Nashville: Abingdon Press, 1994.

Ellul, Jacques. *Prayer and Modern Man.* Translated by C. Edward Hopkins. Seabury Press, 1973.

Evans, Donald. *Spirituality and Human Nature.* Albany: State University of New York, 1993.

Gelineau, Joseph. *The Liturgy Today and Tomorrow.* Paulist Press, 1978.

Hopkins, Gerard Manley. *Poems of Gerard Manley Hopkins.* Edited by W. H. Gardner. Oxford University Press, 1948.

Justin Martyr. "The First Apology of Justin Marytyr." Translated by Bard Thompson (based on critical text of P. Maran in Migne, *patrologiae Graeca,*VI) in *Liturgies of the Western Church,* selected by Bard Thompson. Word Publishing Co., 1961.

Lasch, Christopher. *The Culture of Narcissism: American Life in an Age of Diminishing Expectations.* W. W. Norton & Co., 1979.

Luther, Martin. *The Babylonian Captivity of the Church.* Translated by A. T. W. Seinhäuser, revised by F. C. Ahrens and Abdel Ross Wentz. Reprinted in *Three Treatises.* Fortress Press, 1960.

Nouwen, Henri J. M. *The Living Reminder: Service and Prayer in Memory of Jesus Christ.* Seabury Press, 1977

Oosterhuis, Huub. *Your Word Is Near: Contemporary Christian Prayers.* Translated by N. D. Smith. Newman Press, 1968.

Ramshaw, Gail and Linda Ekstrom. *Words Around the Fire* (1990), *Words Around the Table* (1991), and *Words Around the Font* (1994). Chicago: Liturgy Training Publications.

Saliers, Don E. *The Soul in Paraphrase: Prayer and the Religious Affections.* Seabury Press, 1980. Second edition: OSL Publications, 1991.

Schmemann, Alexander. "Sacrament: An Orthodox Presentation," in *Gospel and Sacrament*. Oecumenica, 1970, published by Augsburg, 1970.

_____. *For the Life of the World*. St. Vladimir's Seminary Press, 1973.

Vogel, Dwight W. *Food For Pilgrims: A Journey With Saint Luke*. Akron, OH: OSL Publications. 1996.